Pilot's Digest of
FAA REGULATIONS

Pilot's Digest of FAA REGULATIONS

by John L. Nelson

MODERN AIRCRAFT SERIES

TAB BOOKS

Blue Ridge Summit, Pa. 17214

FIRST EDITION

SECOND PRINTING—DECEMBER 1977

Copyright 1977 by TAB BOOKS

Printed In the United States
of America

Reproduction or publication of the content in any manner, without express
permission of the publisher, is prohibited. No liability is assumed with respect
to the use of the information herein.

Hardbound Edition: International Standard Book No. 0-8306-9974-0

Paperbound Edition: International Standard Book No. 0-8306-2225-X

Library of Congress Card Number: 72-97774

CONTENTS

FOREWORD

In today's world Federal Aviation Regulations are a basic part of the business of flight. They exist for reasons of safety in air transportation—safety to the pilot, the passenger, and the person on the ground over whose land we travel. The FAR's exist as a means of achieving equity between people in the use of a national resource—our airspace. They are the aviation "law of the land".

Written in the language of the lawyer, Federal Aviation Regulations often require study and interpretation. A purpose of this text is to briefly restate in simple narrative form those regulations commonly employed by the general aviation pilot. However, a more important objective is to outline the manner in which our regulatory system operates. A system does exist for the general aviation pilot to make his voice heard. By understanding the regulatory process we may participate directly in the formation of future Federal Aviation Regulations.

The author wishes to thank the many people who made this book possible, especially the Phoenix FAA General Aviation District Office and TRACON, Barbara Nelson for all of the artwork, Dick Roberts for many helpful suggestions, and daughter Sandy for the final typing. Sincere appreciation is extended to Cessna Aircraft Company, Piper Aircraft Corp., Beech Aircraft Corp., Bellanca Aircraft Corp., Bede Aircraft, Evans Aircraft, King Radio Corp., and EAA for photographs and reference material. The author is indebted to the Electrical and Electronic Engineers, Inc., Washington, D.C. for permission to quote from the text, "The Federal Airways System" by William Jackson and likewise to The Michie Co., Charlottesville, Virginia for legal references from, "The Law of Aviation" by Rowland Fixel. Last, but far from least, sincere thanks are directed to editor Joe Christy for supplying guidance in writing as well as editing of the final product.

J.L.N.

CHAPTER 1
OUR REGULATORY SYSTEM

INTRODUCTION

Federal Aviation Regulations are minimum standards, broad guidelines, desirable procedures, and definitions pertaining to the administration and preservation of our National Airspace. Webster has defined regulation as "the art of reducing to order." And so it is with Federal Aviation Regulations; safe, efficient, and orderly use of the National Airspace directed to fairness and service to the community is the primary objective of our aviation regulatory process. This objective is founded upon democratic principles which recognize public needs as being dominant, and fairness as a stronger requirement than efficiency.

Currently there exist more than 140,000 aircraft operating throughout a network of 12,000 civil airports in the continental United States. Predictions indicate that our air transportation system will expand to 206,000 civil aircraft within the next ten years and double in services to the user. A fair and democratic regulatory process is essential to the continued growth of travel by air.

A "Preflight" Briefing

This text is directed to a brief common language explanation of and rationale for the various Federal Aviation Regulations utilized by the student, private, commercial, and airline transport pilot. Material has been selected from many parts of the Federal Aviation Regulations and condensed to a digest form of the subject; regulatory intricacies and special situations have necessarily been deleted. Should the reader require exact legal definitions, descriptions, or precise detail, it will be necessary to refer directly to the Federal Aviation Regulations (FAR's) for such.

A compromise considered necessary in preparing this document is the limitation of material to Visual Flight Rules (VFR). The subject of Instrument Flight Rules (IFR) is a specialty which is beyond the scope of a discourse on the general subject of FAR's.

A particular objective of this text is to outline the manner in which Federal Aviation Regulations evolve and the large measure of public participation incorporated in the process. In the year 1903, the whole of the National Airspace was shared by two persons, brothers Wilbur and Orville Wright. Today, that same airspace is put to use by more than 800,000 pilots. As a companion in the enjoyment and utilization of our National Airspace we can now ask only our fair share. The challenge at hand is *direct participation* by the airspace *user* in rule making procedures to both *define* and *protect* that "fair share."

HISTORICAL BACKGROUND

Perhaps the first recorded example of an aviation regulatory process-in-action was provided by brothers Jacques and Joseph Montgolfier (acting as air traffic controllers) in providing a takeoff clearance for three stout-hearted aeronauts (a duck, a rooster, and a sheep) for a "once around the patch" balloon flight of eight minutes in the year 1783. Possibly a need for regulation stemmed from early balloonists utilizing rocks for ballast thereby making flight hazardous to persons on the ground. Perhaps the 1861 actions of Lowe in sending the first aerial communication from his balloon signalled the need for regulating the activities of aerial vehicles as observation platforms. Whatever the case may have been, the regulatory process *preceded* the invention of the aircraft by some four years for in 1899 representatives attending the first Hague International Peace Conference acted to prohibit the launching of projectiles and explosives from balloons.

Following the invention of the aircraft and during the period 1905 to 1911, serious consideration was given to registration of aircraft, certification of pilots, and also whether or not property rights and claims of sovereignty of airspace permitted free circulation of aircraft. The first recorded instance of government control of pilot certification and regulation of operations in the United States is found in the Connecticut Act of June 8, 1911.

With the growth of aviation, particularly after World War I, a public need was sensed to control traffic in the vicinity of airports. Initially, the control of aircraft was by men waving arms or flags to indicate to pilots circling the field that a landing was safe—or a take off was permissible. Subsequently, colored directional lights were developed so that they might be focused on a specific aircraft. Pilots learned to look for these lights to give them landing or take off information.

In 1930, at Cleveland, Ohio, an airport traffic control tower was put into operation. This installation proved so successful that several larger municipalities erected towers and staffed them with personnel using light guns and low powered radio equipment. By 1936, approximately 20 cities had followed Cleveland's lead and established similar radio-equipped control towers.

The continuing growth of aviation brought about the need for uniformity in operating procedures. In response, the Civil Aeronautics Act of 1938 was passed which provided for the development of safety provisions related to civil aeronautics. Initially, airport control towers continued to be owned and operated by municipalities. However, personnel employed at these airport traffic control towers were certified by the Civil Aeronautics Authority (CAA) as to theoretical knowledge, physical qualifications, and experience requirements.

Early in 1941, due to the increasing aviation activity brought on by World War II, Congress assigned to the CAA the responsibility for operating certain control towers. Most of the municipally operated traffic control towers were taken over by the CAA on January 1, 1942, with the intention that these towers would be operated by the CAA only for the duration of the war. With the CAA's assumption of these activities, standards were prepared for equipment and operations; tower operators became employees of the Federal government. At that time there were no regulations which required a pilot to comply with instructions issued by a tower controller. Consequently, enforcement of an airport control procedure by the Federal Government was not possible. This condition led to the development of air regulations establishing control zones for governing operation of aircraft operating therein. For the next 20 years, the CAA remained the primary government regulatory agency for U.S. aviation.*

The tremendous growth of aviation during World War II, the introduction of jet aircraft, and the need for a modern electronic system of navigation to accommodate high speed aircraft resulted in a corresponding need for modernization of the aviation regulatory process. A tragic collision of a TWA super constellation and a United Airlines DC-7 over the Grand Canyon on June 30, 1956,

*History of Control Tower Operation and CAA; Jackson, *The Federal Airways System.*

catalyzed the situation and prompted action. The Federal Aviation Act of 1958 resulted, which established the Federal Aviation Agency as the primary regulatory body for both *military and civil aviation* in the United States.

THE SIGNIFICANCE OF FEDERAL LAW

While aviation became a matter for state regulation as early as 1911, the enactment of the Air Commerce Act of 1926, the Civil Aeronautics Act of 1938, and the Federal Aviation Act of 1958, have made aviation law in the United States, its territories and possessions, the law of the land. Exclusive control of aviation by federal law has become increasingly necessary by reason of the increased use of navigable airspace by federally certificated commercial air carriers flying scheduled operations. Furthermore, ground based radio navigation equipment, weather service, air-to-ground communications, instrument landing system, and likewise are provided for by the federal government. Other compelling factors are the extensive use of aircraft by the Army, Navy, and Air Force; the use of commercial aircraft by the Post Office Department in the performance of a national function; the use by foreign aircraft of airspace in the United States; and the protection of airspace over military, naval, and Air Force installations.

It is a well-established principle of constitutional law that where the exercise of control by the federal government is necessary and imperative, and the subject is national in character (such as the regulation of interstate commerce), and furthermore requires uniformity of regulation, the federal government becomes paramount and exclusive. Federal control applies to intrastate as well as interstate traffic. In such cases where there is a state law and also a federal act on the same subject, the latter will control. The United States Supreme Court stated the following with respect to federal control of air commerce:

> Congress has recognized the national responsibility for regulating air commerce. Federal control is intensive and exclusive. Planes do not wander about the sky like vagrant clouds. They move only by federal permission, subject to federal inspection, in the hands of federally certificated personnel and under an intricate system of federal commands. . . . Its privileges, rights and protection, so far as transit is concerned, it owes to the federal government alone, and not to any state government.

Regulation of air commerce and air transit in the airspace above the United States is conceded to be a national responsibility, and the control and regulation of air commerce and air traffic of

all kinds in the United States is recognized to be a federal function.*
In general, state aviation law is limited to matters of taxation, regulation of air carriage wholly within a state, laws concerning liability
for damage to persons and property on the ground by aircraft, and
the power of eminent domain over airports.

THE AVIATION GOVERNMENTAL COMMUNITY

Democratic freedom is a matter of making choices which includes the freedom to share with others in setting up possible
choices. Democratic freedom also implies restrictions in that no
society will allow unlimited choice. Laws, as well as unwritten
codes, may restrict the freedom of the individual in favor of a community standard. The balanced liberty of the United States, sometimes referred to as "ordered freedom," contains the elements of
justice, order, and restraint. Justice is the principle by which each
man is assured the things that belong to him; order is the principle by which peace is maintained; and restraint is the exchange of
unlimited personal freedom for freedom of society as a whole. Our
flying freedom embodies all three basic principles of political freedom:

> Justice: The National Airspace is *shared equally* between gen-
> eral aviation, military aviation, and commercial air carriers.
> (Reflect for a moment as to how many other nations of the
> world grant as much airspace freedom to general aviation as
> that enjoyed within the United States).

> Order: A superb system of airways exist for use by general
> aviation, military aviation, and the air carrier.

> Restraint: Aviation rules and regulations are the "price paid"
> by the individual to obtain his fair share of our National Air-
> space.

Understanding our aviation governmental community is the
first step to understanding Federal Aviation Regulations.

Department of Transportation

The Department of Transportation (DOT) is the parent governmental organization whose responsibilities extend throughout all
forms of transportation in the United States. DOT directs the ef-
forts of the United States Coast Guard, Federal Aviation Administration, Federal Highway Administration, Federal Railroad Administration, Urban Mass Transport Administration, and other
like transportation agencies. In addition to administrative func-

---

*The Significance of Federal Law; Fixel, *The Law of Aviation.*

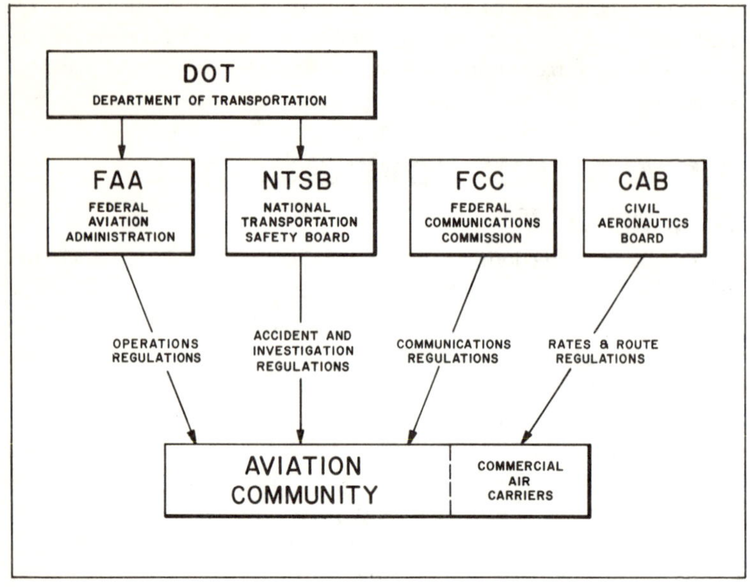

Under the Executive branch of the U.S. Government, the FAA and NTSB are the principal elements of general aviation government.

tions, DOT is responsible for scientific and technological research to advance our national transportation capability in safety, effectiveness, economy, noise abatement, telecommunications, and transportation of hazardous materials.

Federal Aviation Administration

The Federal Aviation Administration (FAA) is the primary governmental authority responsible for the conduct of aviation in the United States. The Federal Aviation Act of 1958 charges the FAA with: regulating air commerce to promote its safety and development; achieving the efficient use of the navigable airspace of the United States; promoting, encouraging, and developing civil aviation; developing and operating a common system of air traffic control and air navigation for both civilian and military aircraft; and promoting the development of a national system of airports. The FAA thus issues and enforces rules, regulations, and minimum standards for the operation, maintenance and manufacture of aircraft, as well as rating and certification of airmen. The agency provides a system for the registration of aircraft, engines, propellers

A classic light twin, the Cessna 310 and its tubocharged counterpart feature seating for 6 adults and cross country speeds up to 221 and 259 mph respectively. With optional fuel cells, the 310 has a range of 1950 miles.

(Photo courtesy of Cessna Aircraft Co.)

and appliances as well as a system for recording aircraft ownership. The FAA may, from time to time, reinspect any civil aircraft, aircraft engine, propeller, and the like as well as re-examine any civil airman. If, as a result of a reinspection, it is determined that safety or public interest so requires, the FAA may amend, modify, suspend, or revoke aircraft type certificates, production certificates, airworthiness certificates, airmen certificates, and other such authorizations as granted by the agency.

The FAA is responsible for the location, construction, installation, maintenance, and operation of our federal system of air navigation. The agency operates and maintains communications equipment, radio teletype circuits and equipment, radio navigation equipment, radar equipment, and equipment at air traffic control towers and Air Traffic Control (ATC) centers.

The management of air traffic operating within our National Airspace system is a primary responsibility of the FAA. To carry out this responsibility the FAA develops air traffic rules and regulations and allocates the use of airspace. It provides for the security control of air traffic to meet national defense requirements. The FAA coordinates with foreign governments in matters of aviation, administers federal aid airport programs, develops specifications for the preparation of aeronautical charts, publishes current information on airways and airport service, and issues technical publications for the improvement of flight safety. The following facilities were provided by the FAA in 1977:

   2   Airports (Washington National and Dulles International)
427   Towers and Combined Station Towers
333   Flight Service Stations
841   Very High Frequency Omniranges (Radio Navigation)
155   Airport Surveillance Radars
 97   Air Route Surveillance Radars
 20   Air Route Traffic Control Centers
 55   Instrument Landing Systems

The FAA is divided into 11 regional offices (including Alaska and Hawaii), and aeronautical center at Oklahoma City, and an experimental center at Atlantic City.

National Transportation and Safety Board

The National Transportation and Safety Board (NTSB) was created as a separate branch of the government by the Department of Transportation Act of 1966. The Safety Board has the authority to investigate, determine the probable cause, and issue reports on all civil aviation accidents; make final cause determination, and report the facts and circumstances related thereto. Authority to investigate accidents of a routine nature is delegated by the NTSB to the FAA. When acting in cooperation with or on behalf of the NTSB, the FAA determines whether or not the aircraft and flight crewmen were properly certificated, the extent to which FAA air traffic control may be involved, whether or not government operated navigation and communication equipment was performing to specified standards, etc. By so doing, FAA lends technical expertise to the various phases of accident investigation and analysis. The determination of probable cause, however, *remains* the *responsibility* of the *NTSB.*

In addition to accident investigations, the NTSB conducts special studies and makes recommendations on matters of aviation safety and accident prevention. Related to the airman, the board reviews (upon request) the suspension, amendment, modification, revocation, or denial of a pilot's certificate. Thus the board acts in the manner of a "higher court," providing the airman a second opportunity to appeal FAA decisions relating to his certificate.

Federal Communications Commission

The Federal Communications Commission (FCC) is responsible for the licensing and regulation of radio broadcasting stations and, in addition, licensing of radio telephone operators. FCC regulations require an airman to have at least a restricted radio telephone operator permit to operate a licensed radio station. Furthermore, FCC regulations require any aircraft which contains a transmitter have an appropriate station license. The aircraft station license must provide for transponder and distance measuring equipment as well as communications transmitters and radar equipment. The FCC, through its Field Engineering Bureau, performs monitoring, inspection, and investigative activities. Periodically the FCC monitors aircraft transmissions to assure that transmitter frequencies are within tolerances and that stations (aircraft) have a valid and current station license.

Civil Aeronautics Board

The Civil Aeronautics Board (CAB) grants authorizations for commercial air carriers to engage in interstate and foreign air transportation over assigned routes. Similarly, it issues permits to foreign air carriers authorizing them to engage in air transportation between the United States and foreign countries. The Board has jurisdiction over tariffs, rates, and fares charged to the public for air transportation. Regulatory action of the CAB is directed to the air carrier and has limited impact on the general aviation pilot.

HOW REGULATIONS COME INTO BEING

Fundamentally, regulations come into being because a *public need exists.* Without a public need there would be no regulations and no regulatory system. Public needs are numerous in quantity and diverse in scope; many result simply from population growth. Consider the following typical examples:

Population Increase: The rapid increase in travel by air has resulted in congestion at major terminals (Washington, New York, Chicago, Los Angeles, Atlanta, and San Francisco). Air traffic studies performed by the FAA and other agencies conclude that the probability of mid-air collisions will become intolerable if an appropriate action is not taken. The result: regulatory action by the FAA to control *all* aircraft in the vicinity of major air terminals; in this case the establishment of Terminal Control Areas (TCA's).

Public Safety: Studies of aviation accidents often disclose cause factors which prompt regulation as a means of reducing accidents. Recent studies performed by the NTSB have revealed that weather is a major cause of general aviation. accidents. The result: regulatory procedures are modified to increase the emphasis on the study of weather as a part of pilot training.

National Defense: Pilot training in modern high speed jet aircraft constitutes a hazard for general aviation and air carriers alike if conducted in common airspace. The result: regulations are enacted to segregate military training operations from general aviation and air carrier traffic. Restricted areas on aviation maps ex-exemplify this type of regulation.

Modernization of Standards: Increased use of the airways and technical advancements in general aviation aircraft necessitate upgrading minimum standards for pilots and air crewmen. A modern single engine aircraft such as the V35B Bonanza is in reality more sophisticated than many combat aircraft of World War II. Similarly, general aviation jet aircraft such as the Learjet or Falcon Fan Jet approach the commercial air carrier in equipment sophistication and performance. The result: FAR-61, Certification of Pilots and Flight Instructors, is modernized. Proficiency requirements are increased for all levels of the aviation pilot community.

The Basic Rule-Making Process: Initiated by a need, a regulation begins life as a petition. An interested person may petition the FAA to issue, amend, or repeal a rule or request an exemption. Petitions must be submitted in duplicate to the FAA, Washington, D.C., 20590; and set forth the text or substance of the rule or amendment proposed, or the rule from which an exemption is sought, or specify the rule that the petitioner seeks to have repealed.

The petitioner must include a complete description of the action being sought and, in the case of an exemption, reasons why safety would not be adversely affected. The FAA may also initiate a rule-making action. In doing so the FAA considers the recommendations of other agencies of the United States and the petitions of interested persons. Petitions for rule-making and related responses are available to the public from the office of the General Counsel of the FAA.

Action on petitions for rule-making may take a number of courses. If the FAA determines that the petition discloses adequate reasons, a Notice of Proposed Rule-Making (NPRM) is issued, or a final rule is adopted, or, if in the public interest, an exemption is granted. If the FAA determines that the petition does not justify instituting rule-making procedures or granting the requested exemption, the petitioner is notified accordingly. For example, con-

After 27 years, the Beech Bonanza is still the classic single engine general aviation aircraft. This model V35B cruises 203 mph at 6500 ft., carries 4-6 persons, has a range of 1,000 miles, and is certificated in the utility category at full gross weight.
(Photo courtesy Beech Aircraft Corp.)

Typical of the corporate aviation fleet, the Beechcraft Hawker 600 offers performance comparable to large transport jet aircraft.
(Photo courtesy Beech Aircraft Corp.)

sider a signficant rule-making procedure such as the modernization of FAR-61. In this case, the FAA, acting on behalf of many
segments of the aviation community, formulates an initial version
of the rule. The proposed rule is advertised to the aviation community by the Federal Register, the aviation news media, and
personal notification (where a party may be directly affected). The
formal means for advertising NPRM's is via the Federal Register.
A Notice of Proposed Rule-Making includes:

1. A statement of the time, place, and nature of the proposed
rule-making proceeding;

2. A reference to the authority under which it is issued;

3. A description of the subjects and issues involved or the substance and terms of the proposed rule;

4. A statement of the time within which written comments
must be submitted and the required number of copies; and

5. A statement of how and to what extent interested persons
may participate in the proceedings.

As an example of this process, the Notice of Proposed Rule-
Making for FAR-61 reads in part:

The Federal Aviation Administration is considering amend-
ing Part 61 to revise the standards for issuing pilot and flight
instructor certificates and ratings. Interested persons are invi-
ted to participate in the making of the proposed rule by submitting such written data, views, or arguments as they may
desire. Communications should identify the regulatory docket
or notice number and be submitted in duplicate to: Federal
Aviation Administration, Office of the General Counsel, Attention: Rules Docket, GC-24, 800 Independence Avenue,
S.W., Washington, D.C., 20591. All communications received
on or before . . . will be considered by the administrator before taking action on the proposed rule. The proposals contained in this notice may be changed in the light of comments
received.

Interested parties do have an opportunity to participate directly in
the rule-making procedures. Part 11 of the Federal Aviation Regulations states:

Each interested person is entitled to participate in rule-making
proceedings by submitting written information, views, or arguments. In addition, he may comment on the original information, views, and arguments submitted by other persons, if,
after receiving them, the administrator considers it desirable.

Part 11 goes on to state:

The rule-making procedure also includes any further procedural steps that best serve the purposes of a particular pro-

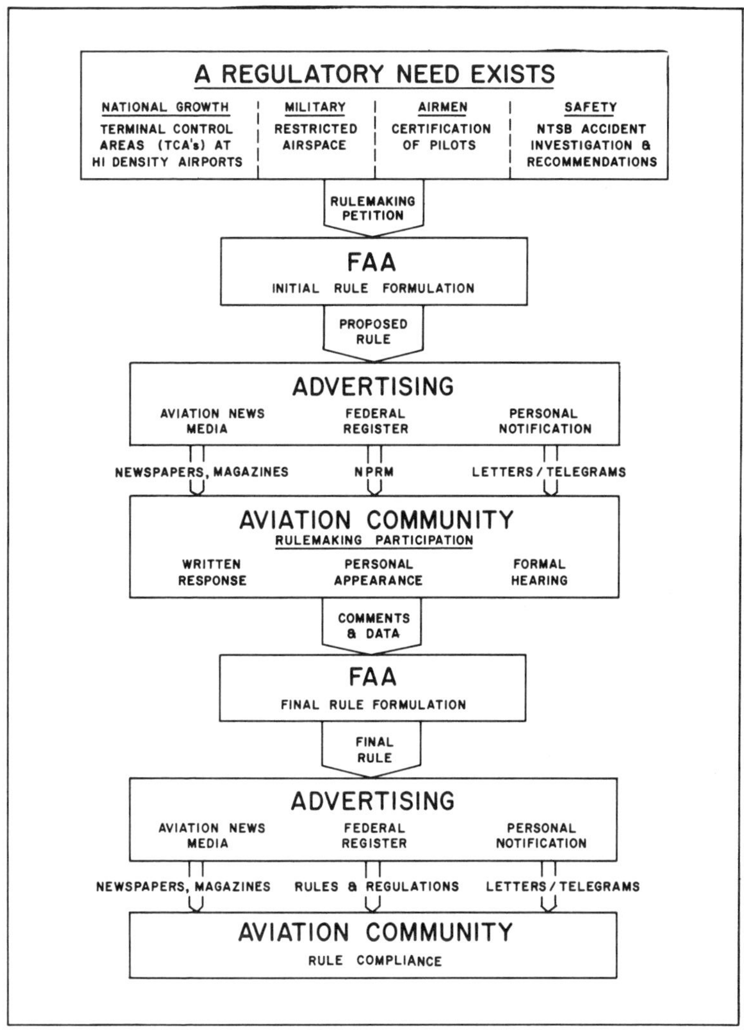

Rule making begins with a public need; proposed regulations are advertised in a formal manner and public opinion solicited. Regulations result after interested parties have forwarded opinions (by letter or in person) and the FAA "weighs" the returns. The objective of the process is to formulate laws that benefit the community in general. In certain special instances aviation laws result from direct congressional action. Laws governing Emergency Locator Transmitters and noise abatement are examples.

ceeding. For example, interested persons may be allowed to make oral arguments, participate in conferences between the administrator or his representative and interested persons and organizations, appear at informal meetings presided over by a designated FAA official at which a stenographic transcript is made, or participate in any other procedure whenever it is desirable and appropriate to assure informed administrative action and adequate protection of private interests.

Is your voice as an individual heard? The answer is indeed yes! The Federal Aviation Administration *is* sensitive to the opinions of the aviation community. Typcially, the results to NPRM's as published in the Federal Register read:

1. Numerous comments have been received in response to the notice of proposed rule-making and changes have been made in the regulation in the light of such comments . . . (FAR 21-2, P5, FR 8464).

2. Finally, in response to some comments, the language of the proposal was changed to specifically include within the term "surface of the airport . . . —etc. ". . . (FAR 91-43, P65, FR 9640).

After public comment and supporting data has been received, the FAA acts to formulate and issue the final rule. Advertising is by the Federal Register and the aviation news media.

Variations on a Theme

The diverse nature of Federal Aviation Regulations leads to variations in the process of rule-making. Rule-making authority is often directed to regional FAA directors, particularly related to airspace assignments and Airworthiness Directives. Rule changes of a routine nature do not require advance public notification. For example, action to modify a transition area at Twenty-Nine Palms, California, reads in part:

Since this change is minor in nature and imposes no additional burden on any person, notice and public procedure hereon is unnecessary.

Similarly, the alteration of a control zone at El Toro, California, as published in the March 18, 1972 issue of the Federal Register reads:

Since this action is less restrictive in nature than currently designated airspace and imposes no additional burden on any person, notice and public procedure hereon is unnecessary.

Upon occasion, regulations such as Airworthiness Directives require immediate attention to a particular problem. As a typical example an Airworthiness Directive related to a rotor blade system reads:

Since it was found that immediate corrective action was re-

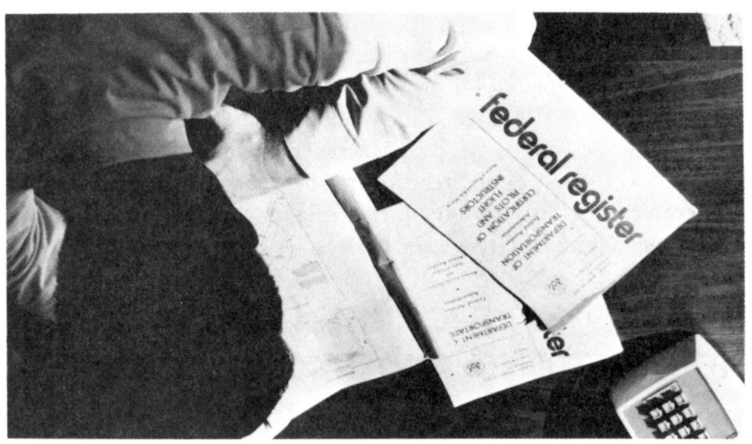

The Federal Register is the formal government publication for advertising regulatory material. Notices of Proposed Rule Making, Rules and Regulations, Airworthiness Directives, and listings of Advisory Circulars are published.

The Piper Seneca features counter rotating engines to eliminate the "critical engine" of conventional twins. Two 200 hp Lycoming power plants provide the muscle to propel the Seneca at speeds up to 195 mph. This light twin will carry 6-7 persons and has a range in excess of 1,000 miles.

(Photo courtesy of Piper Aircraft Corp.)

quired, notice and public procedure thereon was impractical and contrary to the public interest and good cause existed for making the airworthiness directive effective immediately—.

Still another variation on the theme is the issuance of an Advance Notice of Proposed Rule-Making (ANPRM). The purpose of such notification is to propose several courses of rule-making actions and request public reaction to the proposals. This technique is advantageous in shortening the rule-making procedure by inviting public reaction at a very early stage in the rule formulation process.

HOW TO KEEP CURRENT WITH REGULATIONS AND PROCEDURES

Aviation is rich in literature on the subject. The history of aviation has been thoroughly documented. News media widely distribute current events. Even our children speak knowledgeably on future explorations in the fields of aviation and space. What then, about the subject of rules and regulations? Why is the question so often asked, "Where can I obtain a set of regulations—how can I keep current on changes?" The question is indeed valid for in the abundance of aviation literature Federal Aviation Regulations comprise but one small part. The next few paragraphs are devoted to a step-by-step procedure which answers that important question, "Where can I obtain information on regulations—how can I keep current on changes?"

Step I—Publications Catalogs

The initial step to be taken in searching for information is to obtain catalogs which list current aviation publications. The Government Printing Office (GPO) is an excellent source of such material. The following four catalogs are recommended:

The catalog *FAA PUBLICATIONS* contains selected material which is of interest to the public, to pilots, and the aviation industry. Revised editions are issued periodically. The catalog may be obtained free of charge on request by writing:

> Department of Transportation
> Distribution Unit, TAD-484.3
> Washington, D.C.   20590

In your letter, request the text *FAA PUBLICATIONS*. Be sure to include your return name and address, written legibly. A self-addressed mailing label is recommended.

PUBLICATIONS OF THE NATIONAL TRANSPORTA-TION SAFETY BOARD is a listing of printed material of general interest to the public and the transportation industry. It contains a record of all publications issued by the Safety Board. The pamphlet is available free of charge upon request by writing:

> National Transportation Safety Board
> Publications Section
> Washington, D.C.   20591

The FAA issues ADVISORY CIRCULARS to inform the aviation public in a systematic way of non-regulatory material of interest. These excellent documents supplement regulations by providing related material on pertinent subjects such as wake turbulence, aircraft fuel management, radar capabilities and limitations, altitude-temperature effects on aircraft performance, etc. To obtain information on ADVISORY CIRCULARS, write:

> Department of Transportation
> Distribution Unit, TAD-482.3
> Washington, D.C.   20590

Request Advisory Circular 00-1, the ADVISORY CIRCULAR SYSTEM and Advisory Circular 00-2, ADVISORY CIRCULAR CHECKLIST. These documents are available free of charge.

The FAA makes available to the public on a no charge loan basis films, film strips, and audio slide packets on subjects ranging from aviation careers to weather. To obtain information write to the following address for the publication FAA FILM CATALOG:

> Film Library, AC-921
> Federal Aviation Administration
> P.O. Box 25082
> Oklahoma City, Oklahoma   73125

Step 2—Federal Aviation Regulations

FAR's are published in a series of volumes (See Table, next page). To obtain your pilot certificate it is necessary that you study material contained in FAR's 1, 61 and 91, as an absolute minimum. For persons entering aviation on a commercial basis, the information contained in FAR 11, 13, 23, 43, 71, 95, 97, and 135, is recommended. Volumes may be purchased from:

> Superintendent of Documents
> U.S. Government Printing Office
> Washington, D.C.   20402

To expedite getting your publications promptly, send a check, not cash, in the exact amount of the purchase. List the exact name of

ABBREVIATED LIST OF FEDERAL AVIATION REGULATIONS

FAR	TITLE	CAT. NO.	PRICE	FAR	TITLE	CAT. NO.	PRICE
1	Definitions and Abbreviations	TD4.6:1	$ 3.00*	61	Certification: Pilots and Flight Instructors	TD4.6:61	$ 2.90
11	General Rule Making Procedures	TD4.6:11	.55	67	Medical Standards and Certification	TD4.6:67	.50
	Change 1	TD4.6:11/Ch1	.45	71	Designation of Federal Airways, Area Low Routes, Controlled Airspace, and Reporting Points	TD4.6:71	.85
	Change 2	TD4.6:11/Ch2	.40		Change 1	TD4.6:71/Ch1	.30
13	Enforcement Procedures	TD4.6:13	.70	73	Special Use Airspace	TD4.6:73	.40
21	Certification Procedures for Products and Parts	TD4.6:21	3.75*		Change 1	TD4.6:73/Ch1	.30
23	Airworthiness Standards: Normal, Utility, and Acrobatic Category Airplanes	TD4.6:23	3.55*	91	General Operating and Flight Rules	TD4.6:91	11.30*
33	Airworthiness Standards: Aircraft Engines	TD4.6:33	3.00*	93	Special Air Traffic Rules and Airport Traffic Patterns	TD4.6:93	2.45*
35	Airworthiness Standards: Propellers	TD4.6:35	.35	95	IFR Altitudes	TD4.6:95	.50
36	Noise Standards: Aircraft Type and Airworthiness Certification	TD4.6:36	3.00*		Change 1	TD4.6:95/Ch1	.35
37	Technical Standard Order Authorizations	TD4.6:37	5.65*	97	Standard Instrument Approach Procedures	TD4.6:97	.45
39	Airworthiness Directives	TD4.6:39	.35	105	Parachute Jumping	TD4.6:105	.55
43	Maintenance, Preventive Maintenance, Rebuilding and Alteration	TD4.6:43	1.80	135	Air Taxi Operators and Commercial Operators of Small Aircraft	TD4.6:135	2.50
45	Identification and Registration marking	TD4.6:45	.65		Change 1	TD4.6:135/Ch1	.35
					Change 2	TD4.6:135/Ch2	.35
47	Aircraft Registration	TD4.6:47	.85	141	Pilot Schools	TD4.6:141	1.15
49	Recording of Aircraft Titles and Security Documents	TD4.6:49	.45	143	Ground Instructors	TD4.6:143	.45

All FAR's listed are sold on a single sale basis except those noted by a * which are sold on a subscription basis.

the publication you desire. Enclose a self-addressed mailing label if you have no order blank.

NTSB regulations pertaining to the notification and reporting of aircraft accidents are also required as a part of your general knowledge when applying for your pilot certificate. This information is distributed free of charge by writing:

> National Transportation Safety Board
> Publications Section
> Washington, D.C.   20591

Request *PART 830, RULES PERTAINING TO THE NOTIFICATION AND REPORTING OF AIRCRAFT ACCIDENTS, INCIDENTS, AND OVERDUE AIRCRAFT, AND PRESERVATION OF AIRCRAFT WRECKAGE, MAIL, CARGO, AND RECORDS.*

Step 3—Keeping Current

Keeping current is to a great extent a matter of individual need. Let us assume that you are preparing for your FAA written and wish to be current in subjects related to the examination. The FAA publishes EXAM-O-GRAMS which are nondirective in nature and are issued solely as an information service to individuals interested in airman written examinations. EXAM-O-GRAMS are distributed free of charge by writing:

> Department of Transportation
> Federal Aviation Administration
> FSTD, Operations Branch
> P.O. Box 25082
> Oklahoma City, Oklahoma   73125

If you are studying for your private or commercial examination, request the VFR EXAM-O-GRAMS. In the event you intend to obtain your instrument rating request the IFR EXAM-O-GRAMS.

For the average general aviation airman the FAA offers two publications available on a subscription basis as a means of keeping current. The first of these is the FAA AVIATION NEWS. This monthly magazine contains information on rule changes, piloting techniques, special environment flying, aircraft maintenance, etc. The subscription price is currently $4.80 per year. A second publication which provides current information in greater depth is the AIRMAN'S INFORMATION MANUAL. Part I, Basic Flight Manual and ATC Procedures, is issued quarterly at a current cost of $7.60 per year. This manual contains information for both the

Some of the many goverment publications for keeping current; available at no cost are publication listings of the FAA and NTSB, Exam-O-Grams, and most Advisory Circulars.

Hi-performance is the mark of the Super Viking. The Viking cruises at 190 mph (235 mph at 20,000 ft. for the turbo version). Take-off distance is an amazingly short 460 ft. and landing distance only 575 ft.

(Photo courtesy Bellanca Aircraft Corp.)

VFR and IFR pilot. Either publication can be obtained by writing:

Superintendent of Documents
Government Printing Office
Washington, D.C.   20402

Let us assume you are in a business that demands absolute currency of Notices of Proposed Rule-Making, Rules and Regulations, etc. Then the answer is a subscription to the Federal Register. The Register contains regulatory information from the Office of the President, as well as the many executive agencies of the government. The Federal Register is distributed only by the Superintendent of Documents, U.S. Government Printing Office, Washington, D.C. 20402, at a present cost of $5.00 per month, or $50.00 per year, payable in advance.

Need an immediate updating on regulations or procedures? Try the telephone book. Under United States Government, the listing: Department of Transportation, may contain the telephone number for either the Federal Aviation Administration Flight Standards District Office (FSDO), General Aviation District Office (GADO), or Flight Service Station (FSS). These agencies will be able to provide current information on regulations and procedures.

Other ways of keeping current? The aviation news media, magazines, and newspapers perform an excellent service by publicizing current news about regulations, interpretations of procedures, and examples of legal actions related to flying. State aviation agencies often issue newsletters which contain current event information on FAR's. Flight instructors, ground school instructors, and fixed base operators are still another way of keeping current on regulations. In reality regulatory information is abundant and, for the most part, either free or obtainable at a minimal cost.

If you elect to obtain information from the government, expect to practice patience. The Superintendent of Documents receives anywhere from 10,000 to 60,000 requests for publications per day. A wait of six to eight weeks may take place before you receive your documents. In some instances the process can be speeded up by obtaining documents from your local GPO bookstore.

FUTURE TRENDS

Looking to the future of aviation one can only say that its "rate-of-climb" will be phenomenal. During the next ten years combined general and air carrier aviation activity will result in vast increases in traffic to be handled by FAA facilities. Terminal area facilities logged 56.2 million aircraft operations in the year 1970. This total is expected to grow to approximately 130 million operations in 1982! Air carrier and general aviation flying will account for all of the growth in operations as military activities are expected to decline at airports with FAA traffic control towers. As for the general aviation fleet, the total number of aircraft in the year 1971 was 131,000. This number is expected to increase to 206,000 by 1982! Instrument operations are expected to increase from 17.4 million to 32.3 million in 1982, with general aviation as the major contributor to the increase. Pilot briefings, which constitute the largest volume of services and which are primarily for general aviation pilots, are expected to increase over three times their current level. No matter which statistic is examined, the answer is the same—dramatic growth in air transportation.

To accommodate the needs of the future a major air traffic control modernization plan has been enacted. New terminal and enroute radar equipment is being designed to provide more accurate longer range air traffic control coverage. New controller computer and display equipment is being installed. A microwave instrument landing system is being studied and is expected to be operational by the late 1970's. This system will permit the landing of air carrier aircraft in conditions of zero visibility and zero ceiling! Studies are being conducted and legislation is before Congress to establish a national standard for an Airborne Collision Avoidance System. Automatic altitude reporting and air carrier data links will become operational in the not too distant future. Technical answers and equipment are being evolved to handle the predicted 1980 air traffic load. What will be the likely effect on Rules and Regulations?

Predicting the future is difficult at best. However, some events appear certain. The floor of Positive Control will be lowered. The number of Terminal Control Areas will increase and so the number of aircraft under ATC direction. The microwave Instrument Landing System will require development of new procedures for employing the facility. Increased emphasis on the use of transponders is certain. Radar services for the VFR pilot will be increased and improved. Rules, regulations, their number and content will change and increase proportionately. Such is the price of air safety and an equitable distribution of our National Air Space. With this preamble let us begin the study of Federal Aviation Regulations.

CHAPTER 2
THE PILOT

Part I
Pilot Certificates

Flight is an event that renders a sense of satisfaction unique in life's quota of experiences. The world of three dimensional motion offers new vantage points for viewing both the earth and the sky. As with anything worthwhile a significant effort is required to master the theory, practice, and discipline of flight. The sky is fickle in nature, often placid, sometimes hostile. Mastering this medium requires understanding, a bit of skill, and a large measure of determination.

To be certificated as a pilot an applicant must meet the minimum physical standards and aeronautical skill requirements listed in the federal aviation regulations. Three steps are involved in the process. First an applicant must take a physical examination given by an FAA aviation medical examiner. The purpose of this examination is to assure that no defects exist which may be detrimental to flight. Second, an applicant must take a written examination as a measure of his theoretical aeronautical knowledge. Third, an applicant must demonstrate his flight proficiency by a flight test. As we shall see in this chapter the regulations do not require a person to be a physical superman or a mental Einstein. Average abilities are quite adequate to qualify for a pilot certificate.

MEDICAL STANDARDS

Medical standards are divided into three classes. To qualify for a student or private pilot certificate an applicant must pass the requirements for a third class medical certificate. A third class medical certificate is valid for a period of 24 calendar months and represents the minimum physical standards set forth by FAR. The certificate expires on the last day of the calendar month in which it was issued. For example, let us assume that a private pilot obtained a third class medical certificate on Nov. 15, 1977. The certificate would then expire at midnight on Nov. 30, 1979.

A second class medical certificate is required for commercial pilots and flight instructors. This certificate denotes slightly higher minimum physical requirements as logically should be expected of pilots involved in flight for hire. A second class medical certificate is valid for a period of 12 calendar months after the date of issue whereupon it serves as a third class medical certificate for an additional 12 calendar months. Therefore an applicant who qualified for a second class medical certificate on Nov. 15, 1977 may render commercial aviation services until Nov. 30, 1978. Should he wish to continue commercial operations it will be necessary that he renew his second medical prior to this date. However, should he wish to fly only as a private pilot he may do so until Nov. 30, 1979, at which time he must renew his medical if he is to continue flying.

The first class certificate is the most rigorous of the FAA physical examinations. This certificate is intended primarily for air line transport pilots. A first class certificate is valid for a period of six months as a first class certificate, six more months as a second class certificate, and twelve additional months as a third class certificate (24 months in total). The medical certificate is a required companion to the pilot certificate. Both must be carried at all times when performing the duties of a pilot.

Third-Class Medical Certificate
To be eligible for a third-class medical certificate, an applicant must have distant visual acuity of 20/50 or better in each eye separately, without correction; of if the vision in either or both eyes is poorer than 20/50 and is corrected to 20/30 or better in each eye with corrective glasses, the applicant may be qualified on condition he wears glasses while acting as an airman. He must be able to hear the whispered voice at three feet, have no acute or chronic diseases of the internal ear or disturbances in equilibrium. In addition there must be no established medical history or diagnosis of personality disorders, psychosis, alcoholism, drug dependency, epilepsy, unexplained loss of consciousness, convulsive disorders, or other such items. The applicant must have no established medical history of myocardial infarction; or angina pectoris or other evidence of

coronary heart disease that may reasonably be expected to lead to serious heart problems. A history of diabetes that requires insulin or similar agents for control may be disqualifying.

Fundamentally the third class medical is a conventional physical examination whose purpose is to determine possible organic, functional, or other such defects which may make an applicant unable to safely perform the duties of an airman. A further purpose of the certificate is to give reasonable assurance that such will continue to be the case for a period of two years.

Second-Class Medical Certificate

The second-class medical certificate is similar to a third-class certificate except for tolerances being somewhat tighter. To be eligible for a second-class medical certificate an applicant must have distant visual acuity of 20/20 or better in each eye separately, without correction; or at least 20/100 in each eye separately corrected to 20/20 or better with corrective glasses, in which case the applicant may be qualified provided he wears glasses while exercising the privilege of his airman certificate. In addition to normal fields of vision and the ability to distinguish aviation red, green, and white, the applicant must have certain other eye requirements related to bifoveal fixation and vergencephoria. An applicant for a second-class medical certificate must be able to hear the whispered voice at 8 feet with each ear separately. Other requirements are similar to those of the third-class certificate.

First-Class Medical Certificate

The first-class medical certificate embodies all of the requirements of the second-class certificate with additional emphasis on sight, hearing, and heart condition. An applicant for a first-class medical must have distant visual acuity of 20/20 or better in each eye separately, without correction; or at least 20/100 in each eye separately corrected to 20/20 or better with corrective glasses, near vision of at least $V=1.00$ at 18 inches with each eye separately, normal color vision, normal fields vision, and no acute or chronic conditions of either eye that might interfere with the applicant's ability to perform his function as a pilot. The wearing of glasses is permitted. The applicant must have the ability to hear the whispered voice at a distance of at least 20 feet with each ear separately; or demonstrate a hearing acuity of at least 50% of normal in each ear throughout the effective speech and radio range as shown by a standard audiometer. After age 35 an applicant is subject to an electrocardiographic examination to determine his heart condition.

Blood pressure limitations are as shown in the following table:

FIRST CLASS MEDICAL BLOOD PRESSURE LIMITS

Age Group	Maximum readings (reclining blood pressure in mm)		Adjusted maximum readings (reclining blood pressure in mm)	
	Systolic	Diastolic	Systolic	Diastolic
20-29	140	88	---	---
30-39	145	92	155	98
40-49	155	96	165	100
50 and over	160	98	170	100

Blood pressure limits are specified only for the first-class medical certificate. However, as a general guide for the second and third class medical certificates a maximum reading of 170/100 is typical. The person's age, weight, and total physical condition is considered in cases of elevated blood pressure readings.

Medical Limitations

A medical certificate may be issued to an applicant who does not meet the medical standards required by FAR in certain instances. For example, an applicant who is moderately color blind may be able to read the standard aviation red, green, and white signals issued by a tower even though the medical examiners' cards were indistinct as to their color. In a situation of this nature the applicant may apply to the FAA GADO for a practical test of color blindness. A typical test is simply that of the applicant and a local FAA representative "reading" a group of light signals from a tower. If the applicant can successfully determine the color of the signals his operating limitations may be removed; however, should he be unable to do so it is likely that he will be prohibited from flight at night.

Denial of Medical Certificate

Any person who is denied a medical certificate may, within 30 days after the date of denial, apply in writing (in duplicate) to the Federal Air Surgeon, Attention: Chief Aeromedical Certification Branch, Civil Aeromedical Institute, Federal Aviation Administration, P.O. Box 25082, Oklahoma City, Oklahoma 73125, for reconsideration of that denial. If such action is contemplated by an applicant it is important that it be accomplished within 30 days after the date of the applicant's medical certificate denial. Following review by the FAA medical authorities the denial may be upheld, the applicant may be asked to supply additional medical evidence, or simply to demonstrate competence of airmanship (as in the case of a physical handicap). Assuming the latter the FAA may give a combined medical-private or medical-commercial flight test. If the pilot demonstrates competence his certificate may be renewed without waiver; that is, additional "medical" flight tests will not be required.

Medical Examinations: Who May Give.

An FAA physical may be given only by an aviation medical examiner who is specifically designated for the purpose. Your family doctor may or may not be so designated. To obtain a list of qualified medical examiners, in any area, contact the FAA regional director or the FAA GADO. Most fixed base operators, flight schools, flight service stations, or state aviation authorities can provide a list of designated aviation medical examiners.

THE STUDENT PILOT

To obtain a student pilot certificate, a person must be at least 16 years of age, able to read, speak, and understand the English language; and qualify for at least a third-class medical certificate. A combination medical certificate and student pilot certificate will be issued, at your request, by the medical examiner upon the satisfactory completion of your physical examination. Student pilot certificates may be issued by FAA inspectors or designated pilot examiners if the applicant already possesses a valid medical certificate. Since a medical is required prior to solo flight it is really simplest to obtain a student pilot certificate by visiting your aviation medical examiner as the initial step in learning to fly. A combination medical and student pilot certificate is valid for a period of 24 calendar months. The certificate expires at the end of the calendar month in which it was issued two years hence. (For example, a certificate issued on January 2, 1977, will expire at midnight on January 31, 1979).

To solo is to taste adventure. A high point in any pilot's career, the initial solo requires adequate preparation. FAR's specify that, as a minimum, a student pilot be given training in aircraft pre-flight inspection, operating the aircraft engine, taxiing, take-off, landing, traffic pattern procedures, level flight, turns, climbs, glides, stalls, and emergency landings prior to solo. Upon completion of these requirements and demonstration of competence in the control of an aircraft a flight instructor may endorse the student pilot's certificate that the holder is competent to solo. This endorsement must be made prior to the first solo flight and is an endorsement to solo *only in the make and model of aircraft so designated* by the flight

The world's most popular trainer, the Cessna 150 is available in Standard, Trainer, Commuter, and Aerobat models. Powered by an economical 100 hp Continental engine, the Cessna 150 cruises 117 mph at 7,000 ft. and 75% power.
(Photo courtesy Cessna Aircraft Co.)

instructor. A solo endorsement is also required in the student's log book. Except for special cases this solo log book endorsement is valid for a period of 90 days. After this time a student must fly with and have his log book endorsed again by a flight instructor in order to continue solo flight. These endorsements permit student solo only in a local area designated by the flight instructor. A student who is endorsed to solo in one type of aircraft may not solo in another unless his flight instructor has endorsed his student pilot certificate and log book to permit soloing in both aircraft types.

Solo cross country flight is perhaps the high point in student training. Regulations require that, prior to solo cross country flight, a student be given instruction (and demonstrate competence) in basic flight planning elements such as plotting courses, evaluation of weather reports, estimating time on route, and fuel required. In addition competence in cross wind and simulated soft field take-offs and landings, climbing and gliding turns at minimum safe air speeds, and cross country navigation by reference to aeronautical charts is required. Knowledge of safe operating procedures in simulated emergencies such as engine failure, loss of flying speed, marginal visibility, deteriorating weather, becoming lost, and other critical situations is necessary. Skill in conforming with air traffic control instructions by radio and lights, the proper use of two-way radio communications, VFR navigational procedures, and simple maneuvers by reference only to instruments is required prior to solo cross country flight. When a student demonstrates competence in the required skills, a flight instructor may endorse the student's certificate for solo cross country work. A log book cross country endorsement must be made by a certificated flight instructor prior to *each* solo cross country flight. A student must carry his log book on each solo cross country flight. The student's pilot certificate must also be carried on all solo flights. In the event operation of an aircraft radio transmitter is anticipated, a student must obtain an FCC radio telephone operator's permit. This permit can be obtained by sending $4.00 to the Federal Communications Commission in conjunction with FCC Form 753-A. These forms are usually available at flying schools. Once obtained a radio telephone operator's permit is currently valid for life.

Student Pilot Limitations

Federal aviation regulations prohibit a student pilot from carrying passengers, or operating an aircraft for compensation or hire, or in the furtherance of a business. In addition a student pilot is not permitted to make international flights. The purpose of the student pilot certificate is purely for training; extended flight privileges are reserved for those who pass the private pilot examination (or commercial, etc.).

The Written Examination

As a part of the effort in preparing for a private pilot's examination a student must pass a written test on the theory of flight, meteorology, the Airman's Information Manual, FAR's, use of the flight computer, navigation, pre-flight planning, radio procedures, emergency procedures, and basic attitude flying using only aircraft instruments for reference. The minimum passing grade for the written test is 70. In general the written is given at the local FAA GADO and requires typically 3 to 3½ hours to complete. The student need supply only a navigation computer and plotter; text books or notes of any kind are forbidden. The written test is valid for a period of 24 months. In the event an applicant fails a written test he may apply for re-testing after 30 days after the date he has failed the test or upon presenting a statement from an instructor stating he has given additional instruction to the applicant and

A recent addition to the field of trainer aircraft, the American "Trainer" was designed for the beginning pilot. This two-place aircraft employs a 108 hp Lycoming engine and obtains about 20 miles per gallon under normal operating conditions. (Photo courtesy American Aviation).

considers him competent for re-testing. Although ground school is not currently required by FAR many students find this an efficient means of preparing for the written examination. As a minimum the following study materials are recommended in preparation for the private pilot written examination:

1. Pilot's Handbook of Aeronautical Knowledge, AC 61-23A.

2. Private Pilot Written Test Guide, AC 61-32A.

3. Federal Aviation Regulations Parts 1, 61, and 91.

4. Federal Aviation Regulations Written Test Guide AC 61-34A.

5. National Transportation Safety Board Investigation Regulations, Part 430.

6. Private Pilot (Airplane) Flight Training Guide, AC 61-2A.

All items are available from the Superintendent of Documents, Government Printing Office, Washington, D.C. 20402. Item 6 is specially recommended as a means of keeping track of flight training progress.

PRIVATE PILOT CERTIFICATE

To be eligible for a private pilot certificate an applicant must be at least 17 years of age, able to read, speak and understand the English language, hold at least a third-class medical certificate and within 24 months have passed a written examination for the rating of private pilot. In addition the applicant must have at least 40 hours of flight instruction of which 20 hours are solo time. Of the solo time at least 10 hours must be devoted to cross country flight. One cross country flight must include 3 landings at a place more than 100 miles from the point of departure.

Following the student's first solo cross country, FARs require the flight instructor provide at least three hours of training to include maneuvers previously learned, as well as additional maneuvers required for the private pilot test. While the regulations specify a minimum of 40 hours total flight time (35 hours for a certificated flying school), a typical value for the average student is 53 hours. With the increasing complexity of flight we can expect this to approach 60 hours in the near future. The reason is simple. FAR's specify minimum hours only from the standpoint of aeronautical experience. *The real requirement is proficiency, not hours!* Proficiency limits are described in the FAA publication, FLIGHT TEST GUIDE, PRIVATE PILOT, AIRPLANE, SINGLE-ENGINE AC 61-54A. This publication is generally available at aviation flight schools.

When a person has acquired the necessary qualifications and has obtained a written recommendation for a flight test from an appropriately rated flight instructor he may apply for the private pilot flight test. The flight test can be taken at any FAA GADO or from a designated pilot examiner. There is no charge for flight tests when conducted by an FAA inspector; however, designated pilot examiners are entitled to charge a reasonable fee. A private pilot test consists of three phases, an oral examination, a basic piloting technique, and a cross country test. FAR's require that an applicant perform the following procedures and maneuvers:

1. Phase I—Oral Operational Test:
An applicant will be required to present and explain aircraft registration, airworthiness and equipment documentation, as well as airplane log books and airworthiness inspection reports. To determine that the applicant knows what performance and operating information is important he is required to demonstrate a practical knowledge of aircraft performance para-

meters, range, operation, weight and balance, etc. In addition the oral test covers aircraft pre-flight procedures and the use of radio for voice communications.

2. Phase II—Basic Piloting Technique Test:
The objective of Phase II is to evaluate the student's flying skill. A demonstration of pre-flight procedures, taxiing, normal and cross wind take-offs and landings, climbs, level flight, descents, and flight at minimum controllable speeds is required. Stalls and stall recovery, 720 degree steep turns about a point, full stall landings, short and soft field take-offs and landings, and engine out emergency landings are required.

3. Phase III—Cross Country Flight Test:
The objective of this phase of testing is to determine whether the applicant can effectively prepare for a cross country flight in a reasonable period of time and furthermore conduct such in a safe expeditious manner using normally available aids and facilities. Before take-off for the flight test, the applicant will be requested to plan a cross country flight to a point at least two hours cruising range distance in the airplane to be used for the test. At least one intermediate stop will normally be included. The student is expected to procure pertinent available weather information, plot the assigned course, establish check points, estimate flying time, and fuel requirements. The use of the Airman's Information Manual for reference information and a flight computer for dead reckoning computations is expected.

As a part of the flight test the examiner will request the student demonstrate cross country flying ability by following a designated course, the use of radio aids in VFR navigation, and instrument flight. During simulated instrument flight the student must be able to recover from the start of a power-on spiral, recover from the approach to a climbing stall, and execute normal turns of at least 180 degrees to within plus and minus 20 degrees of a pre-selected heading. Shallow climbing turns to a pre-determined altitude, shallow descending turns at reduced power to a pre-determined altitude, and straight and level instrument flight is required.

During a flight test the examiner acts in the capacity of an observer; the student is pilot in command. The examiner simply poses the problem, the student is responsible to demonstrate the correct response. A successful flight test is denoted by obvious mastery of the aircraft, the outcome of a maneuver must never be in doubt. A student who fails a flight test may apply for a re-test upon presenting a statement from his flight instructor that he has been given additional instruction and the flight instructor now considers the applicant ready for re-testing.

COMMERCIAL PILOT CERTIFICATE

To qualify for a commercial pilot certificate the person must be at least 18 years of age, be able to read, speak, and understand the English language, hold a valid first or second class medical certificate, and have the aeronautical experience required. In addition, to take the commercial flight test, an applicant must have passed within 24 months the commercial pilot written examination and have a written recommendation from a flight instructor stating that he has qualified for a commercial flight test. An instructor's recommendation for a flight test is valid for 60 days.

Aeronautical experience required for the commercial certificate consists of a minimum of 250 hours of total flight time including at least 100 hours of flight time in powered aircraft of which at least 15 are solo. In addition, 100 hours of flight time must be as pilot in command including a minimum of 50 hours of cross country time. Cross country experience must include takeoffs and landings from two different airports under two way radio instruction from an airport tower as well as one cross country flight of at least 350 miles including three landings, one of which is at least 150 miles from the point of departure. In preparation for the commercial flight test a student must have a minimum of 10 hours of instrument flight instruction and 10 hours of flight instruction devoted to maneuvers required for the commercial pilot flight test. To qualify for night flight under ICAO (International Civil Aviation Organization) requirements, an applicant must have at least 5 hours of flight time at night, including at least 10 take-offs and 10 landings as pilot in command.

The commercial pilot flight test is conducted in four phases: an oral examination, basic flying techniques, precision flight maneuvers, and a cross country flight. The test is similar in principle to the private pilot examination except that a greater depth of knowledge, accuracy, and flying skill is expected. In addition the applicant must demonstrate the required precision flight maneuvers. These maneuvers consist of gliding spirals, on-pylon eights, lazy eights, steep turns, chandelles, maneuvering at minimum controllable air speed, and stalls from all normally anticipated flight attitudes with and without power. Accuracy landings within 200 feet beyond a designated mark are also required. Proficiency requirements are listed in the FAA publication FLIGHT TEST GUIDE, COMMERCIAL-PILOT-AIRPLANE, AC 61-55A.

CHAPTER 2—THE PILOT (CONTINUED)

Part II
General Requirements

PILOT CERTIFICATES

Upon the successful completion of a flight test the pilot will be issued a temporary certificate which is valid for a period of 90 days. During this time the FAA Airman Certification Branch at Oklahoma City will issue a permanent pilot certificate. Pilot certificates for the private and commercial ratings are permanent in nature and are kept valid by the renewal of the associated medical certificate. At any time a person acts as pilot in command he must have in his possession a current pilot certificate and medical certificate. If requested a pilot shall present either or both to the FAA, the NTSB, or any federal, state, or local law enforcement officer for inspection. The holder of any certificate that is suspended or revoked shall, upon request, return it to the FAA. Flight instructor certificates and student pilot certificates automatically expire at the end of the 24th calendar month after the month in which they were issued.

To replace a lost or destroyed pilot certificate write to the Department of Transportation, Federal Aviation Administration, Airman Certification Branch, P.O. Box 25082, Oklahoma City, Oklahoma 73125. Include your name, permanent mailing address, social security number, date and place of birth, and any available information regarding the grade, number, and date of issue of the certificate. A check or money order for $2.00 payable to the FAA is required. In a similar fashion an application for a replacement of a lost or destroyed medical certificate is made by letter to the Department of Transportation, Federal Aviation Administration, Civil Aeromedical Institute, Aeromedical Certification Branch, P.O. Box 25082, Oklahoma City, Oklahoma 73125. A check or money order for $2.00 is likewise required.

AIRCRAFT AND PILOT RATINGS

As a means of subdividing the various kinds of airplanes, FAR's use the words category, class, and type. Unfortunately, the same three words are also used for subdividing airmen ratings. Applied to an aircraft the word category describes the intended use of the vehicle with class being a descriptive modifier. Applied to a pilot the word category describes the fundamental airborne device involved with class as a descriptive modifier. To clarify the matter the following table lists category, class, and type nomenclature applicable to the aircraft and to the pilot.

ITEM	CATEGORY	CLASS	TYPE
Aircraft	Transport Normal Utility Acrobatic Limited Restricted Experimental Provisional	Airplane Rotocraft Glider Balloon Landplane Seaplane	Cessna 150 Beech B19 Etc.
Pilot	Airplane Rotocraft Glider Lighter-than-Air	Single-Eng. Land Single-Eng. Sea Multi-Eng. Land Multi-Eng. Sea Gyroplane Helicopter Airship Free Balloon	Cessna 150 Piper 140 Etc.

Type Ratings

A pilot's certificate describes the category, class, and type of aircraft the holder is rated to fly. For example a commercial pilot's certificate may read "Airplane, multi engine-land, Boeing 707". Thus the certificate clearly describes the category, class, and type of aircraft that the pilot is rated to fly. A private pilot may have a certificate which reads "Airplane, single engine-land". In this instance only the category and class of aircraft are specified. Type ratings are required for large aircraft (over 12,500 pounds), turbojet powered aircraft, and certain helicopters. The absence of a type

A two to four place aircraft, the Beech Sport B19 cruises 131 mph at 7,000 ft. and offers a range of 767 miles. The Sport B19 is certificated in the utility category at a gross weight of 2,030 lbs. and in the normal category at 2,250 lbs.

(Photo courtesy of Beech Aircraft Corp.)

rating on a certificate indicates the pilot is authorized to operate only small aircraft for which no type rating is required. In order to obtain a type rating an applicant must hold or concurrently obtain an instrument rating, possess the required aeronautical experience, and demonstrate proficiency by a flight test. Since large aircraft often differ in their operating limits and techniques, type ratings are employed to require and test for pilot proficiency in the specific aircraft of concern.

Class Ratings

The class rating is an item of greater interest to the general aviation pilot than the type rating. For example, a pilot whose certificate reads "Airplane, single engine-land," wishes to transition to a multiengine-land aircraft. In this instance a class rating is involved. In order to obtain a class rating an applicant must have made at least five take-offs and landings in the aircraft in which he seeks a rating, in solo flight or as the only manipulator of the controls accompanied by a pilot rated to carry passengers in that aircraft. In addition he must obtain a flight instructor's written recommendation and pass a flight test in the aircraft for which he desires a class rating. The flight test may be given by an FAA examiner or a designated pilot examiner and, for all practical purposes, is similar to the private or commercial flight test (depending upon the level the applicant seeks).

SOLO FLIGHT

A pilot may fly a small aircraft solo provided he meets one of the following conditions:

1. He holds a category and class rating for that aircraft.

2. He has soloed in that category and class of aircraft prior to December 16, 1965.

3. He has made at least three take-offs and landings in that category and class of an aircraft as the sole manipulator of the controls, while accompanied by a pilot who is entitled to carry passengers in that aircraft or is operating under an authorization from the FAA.

These requirements do not apply to the student pilot or in cases of operating an experimental or provisional type certificated aircraft. A pilot whose certificate reads "Airplane, single engine-land" may currently fly solo in any single engine-land aircraft less than 12,500 pounds gross weight. However, after November 1, 1974 flight instruction in high performance aircraft (over 200 hp.) will be required to act as pilot-in-command thereof.

CARRYING PASSENGERS, RECENCY OF EXPERIENCE

To carry passengers a pilot must have a category and class rating for the aircraft in which he intends to carry passengers as well as meet FAR requirements relating to recency of flight experience. FAR 61.47 states that, within the preceding 90 days, a pilot must have made at least five take-offs and five landings to a full stop in an aircraft of the same category, class, *and type* to act as pilot in command of an aircraft carrying passengers. This FAR must be read carefully for the word type now applies to small aircraft. Thus, if a pilot wishes to carry passengers in a Cessna 172 he must have made 5 take-offs and landings within 90 days in a Cessna 172. Should he wish to carry passengers in a Cessna 182 he must likewise make five take-offs and landings in that aircraft within a period of 90 days. If he wishes to carry passengers at night he must have made the five landings and takeoffs within the past 90 days during the night season. Insofar as recency of experience is

Used for primary and instrument training, the Cherokee 2+2 Cruiser provides either two or four place seating. The aircraft is unique in that air conditioning is offered as an option.
(Photo courtesy of Piper Aircraft Corp.)

concerned, night is defined as beginning one hour after sunset and ending one hour before sunrise. The pilot is not required to perform five take-offs and landings both day and night in all types of aircraft in which he may carry passengers; night experience is transferrable. As an example let us take the case of a flight instructor that regularly gives instruction in a Cessna 150, a Cessna 172, a Cessna 182, and a Cessna 310. So long as he makes five take-offs and landings in one of the four aircraft at night he is considered current to carry passengers in the other three types of aircraft at night. Of course this assumes that he has completed the required number of landings and take-offs in the remaining three aircraft during the day season.

PILOT LOG BOOKS

Flight time used to meet experience requirements for any pilot certificate or rating, or to meet recent flight experience requirements must be shown by a reliable record. The logging of other flight time is not required. Needless to say fraudulent or intentionally false entries to show compliance with certification requirements are prohibited.

CHANGE OF ADDRESS

In the event a pilot changes his permanent mailing address he is required to notify the FAA within 30 days. New address information should be forwarded to the Department of Transportation, Federal Aviation Administration, Airmen Certification Branch, P.O. Box 25082, Oklahoma City, Oklahoma 73125.

AFTER NOVEMBER 1, 1974

As Tennyson wrote, "The old order changeth, yielding place to the new." Effective November 1, 1974 a biennial flight review will be required of all pilots not engaged in airline or commercial operations where the FAA already requires periodic flight checks. The review will include an examination of a pilot's knowledge of FAR's and flying skills appropriate to the pilot's certificate. The purpose of the review is to assure that at least once every 2 years each pilot rides with a competent instructor who can comment on his ability. The flight review *is not* a flight check! The person giving the review need only certify (in the pilot's logbook) that the pilot has successfully accomplished the review—an endorsement of the pilot's competency is not required. Flight reviews must be accomplished prior to November 1, 1974. Other important regulatory changes are:

1. Applicants for written tests must show evidence of having completed an appropriate course of study.

2. An applicant for a private pilot certificate must have at least 20 hours of dual instruction including 3 hours at night to qualify for night flight privileges.

3. An applicant for a commercial certificate must have 250 hours of flight time plus an instrument rating to qualify for unrestricted flight privileges.

4. To act as pilot-in-command of a high performance aircraft that has more than 200 hp., or that has a retractable landing gear, flaps, and a controllable pitch propeller a private or commercial pilot must obtain flight instruction in such an aircraft. Instruction is not required if the pilot has logged pilot-in-command time in such aircraft before November 1, 1973.

CHAPTER 3
THE AIRCRAFT

Part I
The Certification Process

If ever variety was abundant, aviation was deeply blessed in its dawning moments. Early experimenters designed, constructed and flew (sometimes) an almost endless mixture of airplane configurations. Fuel sources included steam, electricity, diesel fuel, and gasoline. Building materials ranged from paper, wicker, and bam-

A most unusual aircraft, the Burnelli CBY was built to a joint Canadian, British, and United States specification. Powered by two R-1830 engines, the aircraft first flew in 1945; cruise speed 264 mph at 7,000 ft. This 17,500 lb. aircraft once carried a payload of 27,500 lbs.!   (Photo courtesy of Dale Hamilton.)

boo to duraluminum. Slowly as the limits of technology increased, the evolutionary process of selecting the "fittest of the breed" laid the ground work for standardization of airplanes and motive power. The magnificent helium and hydrogen filled dinosaurs of the lighter-than-air age were relegated to extinction. The biplane gave way to the monoplane; the pusher to the tractor; and the radial engine bowed to the turboprop and turbo jet. The flying wing designs of John Northrop, the lifting body fuselage of Burnelli, and the Canard aircraft no longer traverse our airways. The airplane has become standardized in shape, motive power, quality, operation, and safety.

Title VI of the Federal Aviation Act of 1958 states that the FAA shall be empowered to regulate civil aircraft in air commerce by prescribing minimum standards governing the design, materials, workmanship, construction, and performance of aircraft, aircraft engines, and propellers as may be required in the interest of safety. Furthermore, the FAA is empowered to prescribe reasonable rules and regulations and minimum standards governing: (a) the inspection, servicing, and overhaul of aircraft, aircraft engines, propellers, and appliances; (b) the equipment and facilities for inspection, servicing, and overhaul; (c) periods for, and the manner in which inspection, servicing, and overhaul shall be made, including provision for examination and reports by properly qualified persons. Fundamentally, the FAA is granted "standardization" authority; an authority that extends from design concept throughout production, testing, and operation of an aircraft during its total life span.

GENERAL PROGRAM OF AIRCRAFT CERTIFICATION

The program of aircraft certification provides for the issuance of a *type certificate* which signifies a design as satisfactory, a *production certificate* which maintains a design through the process of manufacture, and an *airworthiness certificate* which denotes to the owner that his aircraft meets the requirements specified by the original type certificate. Since the airworthiness certificate is renewed by periodic maintenance inspections, the standards set forth by the original type certificate are theoretically retained throughout the life of the aircraft.

The purpose of the certification program is to govern standards required in the interest of public safety. This is accomplished by requiring *demonstrated proof of performance* to qualify for a certificate. Design techniques, material choices, and production processes are left to the manufacturer or individual so long as basic

The Northrop XB-35 Flying-Wing. Powered by four Pratt & Whitney R-4360 engines, this unique aircraft employed tandem contrarotating propellors. The aircraft was designed as a military vehicle and first flew on June 25, 1946. A jet version, the YB-49, made its maiden flight 16 months later.
(Photo courtesy of the Smithsonian Institute.)

safety standards are met. The program provides for the individual in the process of constructing an experimental aircraft of unique design as well as the manufacturer who may produce hundreds of look-a-like aircraft; either may obtain an airworthiness certificate for his final product.

TYPE CERTIFICATES

Type certificates are granted for aircraft, engines, propellers, and appliances (radios, instruments, etc). Aircraft type certificates denote weight and balance limits, propeller speed and pitch limits, stall speed limits, take-off, climb, landing and spin characteristics. Controllability and maneuverability limits are specified as well as ground handling characteristics. Structural safety factors are specified for flight loads that act upon the various surfaces of the aircraft. Aircraft fuel, oil, cooling, induction, exhaust, power plant, instrumentation, electrical, hydraulic, lighting, oxygen, and other like subsystems are defined. In essence a type certificate is a *formal specification* which describes *all vital aircraft characteristics* including the properties of its subsystems.

Type Certificate, Normal, Utility, Aerobatic, and Transport Category Aircraft

Type certificates are granted for normal, utility, aerobatic, and transport categories of aircraft provided design data and test reports demonstrate that the product meets applicable airworthiness and aircraft noise requirements. The normal category type certification is limited to airplanes intended for non-aerobatic operation. Non-aerobatic operation includes maneuvers incident to normal flight, stalls (except whip-stalls), lazy eights, chandelles, and steep turns in which the angle of bank is not more than 60 degrees. The utility category provides for airplanes intended for *limited* aerobatic operation. Utility category aircraft may be certified for spins (if approved for the particular type of airplane), lazy eights, chandelles, and steep turns in which the angle of bank is more than 60 degrees. Some utility aircraft (including popular models) are extremely limited in spin recovery characteristics! Check with your local GADO to determine the exact limitations of your aircraft *before* entering into any maneuver that may result in an accidental spin! The aerobatic category is the only category provided for aircraft intended for use without restriction (other than those resulting from certification flight testing).

Another distinction between normal, utility, and aerobatic categories is the limit maneuvering load factor. For aircraft in the normal category that do not exceed a gross weight of 4,117 pounds, the positive limit maneuvering load factor is 3.8 G's. Aircraft in excess of this weight are permitted a lower positive G limit depending upon weight but not less than 2.1 G's. Utility category airplanes must accommodate a positive limit load factor of 4.4 G's. The positive limit load factor for aerobatic category aircraft is 6.0 G's. Negative load limit factors are required to be at least 40% of the positive load factor for the normal and utility categories and 50% of the positive load limit factor for aerobatic category aircraft. The limit load factors represent the minimum strength of the weakest part of the aircraft when subjected to G loadings from turbulence, steep turns, dive recovery, and the like. These loadings apply with flaps up only. With flaps down positive G loadings are reduced by a factor of 50% and negative G loadings are reduced to zero!

Type Certificate, Restricted Category Aircraft

Aircraft intended for special purpose operations may be granted a restricted category certificate if it can be shown that the aircraft is safe when operated under the limitations prescribed for its intended use. Such aircraft are not permitted to operate for reasons other than the special purpose for which the aircraft was certificated. Crew members are limited to persons essential to the special purpose function. Restricted category civil aircraft may not operate over densely populated areas, in congested airways, or near a busy airport where passenger transport operations are conducted. Typical of special purpose operations for which a restricted type certificate may be granted are:

1. Agricultural spraying, dusting, and seeding, and predatory animal control.
2. Forest and wild life conservation.
3. Aerial surveying (photography, mapping, oil, and mineral exploration).
4. Patroling (pipeline, powerlines, and canals).
5. Weather control (cloud seeding).
6. Aerial advertising (sky writing, banner towing, airborne signs and public address systems).

Type Certificate, Provisional Category Aircraft

Provisional type certificates are *temporary* certifications issued for a limited time special purpose operation; 24 months for a class I certificate and 12 months for a class II certificate. The provisional type certificate is typically granted for:

1. Demonstration flights by a manufacturer for prospective purchasers; as in the case of a foreign built aircraft being demonstrated in the United States.
2. Market surveys by a manufacturer.
3. Flight checking of instruments, accessories, and equipment

that do not affect the basic airworthiness of the aircraft.

4. Service testing of the aircraft.

Only persons who have a proper interest in the special purpose operation being conducted or who are specifically authorized by the manufacturer and/or the FAA may be carried in a provisionally certificated aircraft.

Other Type Certificates

The FAA grants type certificates for gliders, surplus military aircraft, and various imported products. Supplemental type certificates are issued to update an original type certificate or extend its use (as in the case of a new model of an existing aircraft). The holder of a type certificate is required to report any defect in any product or part manufactured that could result in a structural failure, flight control system malfunction, engine failure, propeller failure, fire, brake failure, or other hazardous conditions.

AIRWORTHINESS CERTIFICATES

Standard airworthiness certificates are granted aircraft in the normal, utility, aerobatic, and transport categories at the time of manufacture and remain current provided maintenance and alterations to an aircraft are performed in accordance with FAR 43 (Maintenance, Preventative Maintenance, Rebuilding and Alterations) and FAR 91 (General Operating Flight Rules).

Special airworthiness certificates are granted to restricted, limited, provisional, and experimentally qualified aircraft. These certificates remain in effect as long as prescribed maintenance operations are conducted with the exception of experimental certificates which are valid for one year after the date of issue or renewal (unless a shorter period is prescribed by the FAA).

The experimental airworthiness certificate deserves special consideration for under this certificate amateur built aircraft are certified airworthy. The growth of the amateur built aircraft movement under the direction of the Experimental Aircraft Association is one of the truly significant events occurring in aviation today. This revitalization of flying at the grass roots level was made possible by changes in federal law which extended airworthiness certification to amateur built aircraft (circa 1950). As a result amateur built aircraft are competing with—and often exceeding—performance capabilities of production aircraft! At present amateur built aircraft hold the world championship for aerobatics and numerous racing titles. It is interesting to note that NASAD (Na-

Symbol of the Experimental Aircraft Association, this fully aerobatic aircraft, the Acro Sport, is typical of amateur built aircraft. Plans are available from EAA, P.O. Box 229, Hales Corners, Wisconsin 53130.

(Photo courtesy of EAA and Dick Stouffer.)

Performance is the word to describe the BD-5. This remarkable amateur built aircraft is capable of 200 mph flight. A truly unique design, the BD-5 is available in kit form from Bede Aircraft, Inc., P.O. Box 706, Newton, Kansas 67114.

(Photo courtesy of Bede Aircraft.)

tional Association of Sport Aircraft Designers) has recently adopted a system of *voluntary minimum standards* for the specification, fabrication, and flight test of amateur built aircraft.

Experimental airworthiness certificates are awarded amateur built aircraft on the basis that the major portion of the fabrication and assembly is conducted by persons for their own education or recreation. FAA inspections are required prior to enclosing the aircraft framework and following final assembly of the craft. Typically, 50 hours of flight test is initially required, to be conducted in a specified test area. The purpose of the flight test program is to demonstrate that the aircraft is controllable throughout its normal range of speed and maneuvers; furthermore, that the aircraft has no hazardous operating characteristics or design features. Assuming the aircraft meets minimum safety criteria from the standpoint of design and workmanship and successfully passes the assigned flight test program, an experimental airworthiness certificate will be issued. Experimental aircraft are not permitted to carry persons or property for compensation or hire. Furthermore, such aircraft may operate under VFR day-only conditions unless otherwise specified by FAA. Except for take-offs and landings, operation of an aircraft with an experimental certificate is not permitted over a densely populated area or in a congested airway. Passengers must be advised of the experimental nature of the aircraft.

In addition to amateur built aircraft, experimental airworthiness certificates are granted for research and development purposes, demonstrating compliance with regulations, crew training, exhibitions, motion pictures, television, air racing, and market surveys. Experimental aircraft may employ non-conventional materials, unique fabrication techniques, and engines that are not type certificated. Amateur built aircraft have employed automotive engines, ground power unit engines, and, at least in one case, multiple go-cart engines for power.

Limited Airworthiness Certificates

Limited airworthiness certificates are specialized airworthiness authorizations typically granted for unique situations such as the conversion of an ex-military aircraft to civil use.

INSTRUMENTATION AND AVIONICS EQUIPMENT STANDARDS

Just as the type certificate is a standard for an airframe, an engine, or propeller, the Technical Standard Order (TSO) is the standard for aircraft instrumentation and avionics equipment. The purpose of the TSO is to insure that an article will operate satisfactorily and accomplish its intended purpose under specified use conditions. In order to obtain a TSO authorization a manufacturer must demonstrate that his device, (a transponder for example) meets minimum performance requirements under the environmen-

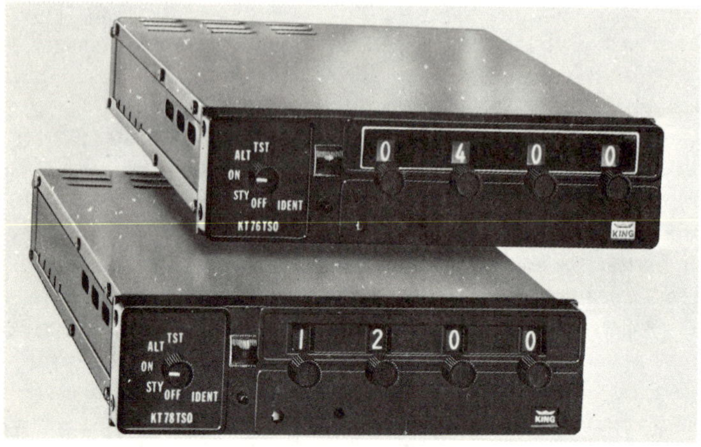

Typical of general aviation radio equipment which meets FAA Technical Standard Orders (TSO's) are the King KT 76 hi-altitude transponder, KT 78 low altitude transponder, and KX 175 Nav/Comm. FAR's require that all transponder equipment used after July 1, 1975 meet TSO standards.

(Photo courtesy of King Radio Corp.)

tal conditions specified. A manufacturer of an article for which a TSO authorization has been issued may market the device providing that he maintains an adequate quality control system, a current file of complete technical data and records, permits the FAA to inspect the article as well as the manufacturer's facilities, and reports any failures, malfunctions, or defects that may result in a hazardous situation to the user. The TSO is not an ironclad guarantee of equipment quality and reliability. However, it goes a long way toward providing the dependable service all airmen desire of their avionics equipment.

At the present time only certified air carriers are required to equip their aircraft with TSO approved equipment. An exception is the transponder. Since improperly operating transponders raise havoc with the ATC system, general aviation aircraft will be required to use only transponders that conform to TSO specifications by July 1, 1975. Furthermore, transponder equipment will be subject to an annual operational test beginning January 1, 1974.

CHAPTER 3—THE AIRCRAFT (CONTINUED)

Part II
Aircraft Ownership and Maintenance

AIRCRAFT OWNERSHIP

The ownership of an aircraft as an individual, a partnership, a club, or as a corporation is becoming an increasingly common occurrence. Aircraft ownership is in many respects similar to ownership of an automobile. Both are subject to registration, licensing, "rules of the road", and accident reporting procedures. Furthermore, in many states automobiles are required to have an annual inspection for safety purposes just as aircraft are required to have an annual inspection. The primary differences between the two are the requirements for controlled maintenance of aircraft and registration by the federal rather than the state government. As an owner of an aircraft, you are responsible for the following:

1. Registering and recording your aircraft title in accordance with Parts 47 and 49 of the Federal Aviation Regulations.

2. Keeping your airworthiness certificate current by having your aircraft inspected annually and complying with applicable AD notices.

3. Maintaining your aircraft and avionics equipment in an airworthy condition.

4. Assuring that all maintenance is properly recorded (in both the engine and airframe log books).

5. Keeping abreast of current regulations concerning the operation and maintenance of your aircraft.

6. Notifying the FAA Aircraft Registry immediately of any change of permanent mailing address or of the sale or export of your aircraft.

AIRCRAFT PURCHASE AND OPERATION

In buying an aircraft there is no substitute for examining the aircraft records to obtain a history of the ownership of the aircraft and to determine if there are any outstanding liens or mortgages—before purchase! This procedure will help avoid delay in registering an aircraft, and the headaches many aircraft purchasers have suffered because they failed to take this one important step. Naturally the purchase of an aircraft from a reputable distributor or dealer is desirable. However, even these people may fail to determine the true title status of an aircraft.

When buying a used aircraft, it is desirable to have the aircraft inspected by a qualified person or facility *before* signing a sales agreement. The condition of the aircraft and the state of its maintenance records can be determined by persons knowledgeable on that particular make and model. These include a certificated Airframe and Power plant (A & P) mechanic or an approved repair station. A check of public records may likewise be of value. All aircraft public records are maintained by the FAA and are on file at the following address:

> Department of Transportation
> FAA Aeronautical Center
> Aircraft Registration Branch
> AC-250, P.O. Box 25082
> Oklahoma City, OK 73125

As a minimum, the purchaser of either a new or a used aircraft may expect to receive at time of purchase the following legal documents:

1. Bill of Sale (Aircraft Title).

2. Airworthiness certificate.

3. All aircraft and engine log books.

4. A list of equipment installed.

5. Weight and balance data.

6. Appropriate maintenance manual, service letters, bulletins, etc.

7. Airplane flight manual or operating limitations.

The following documents must be carried aboard the aircraft at all times:

1. Airworthiness certificate (must be displayed within the aircraft.

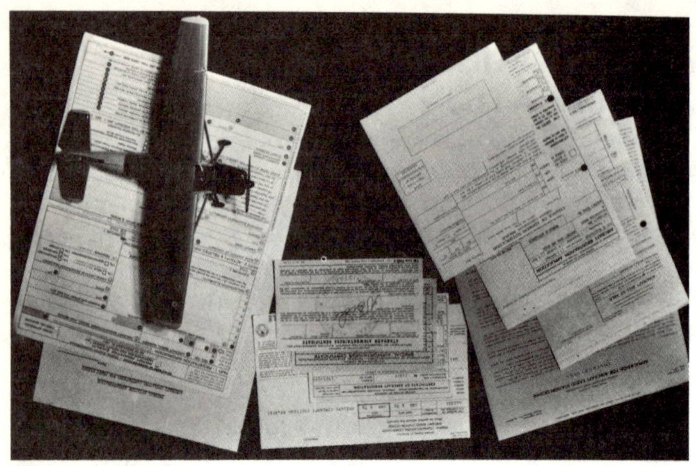

Every aircraft must carry an Airworthiness Certificate, and a Certificate of Registration. An aircraft Registration Eligibility, Identification, and Activity Report must be filed annually. An internal revenue tax (IRS Form 4638) is also an annual obligation.

2. Certificate of registration.

3. Operations limitations and/or airplane flight manual. For aircraft over 6,000 pounds certificated gross weight an FAA approved airplane flight manual is required; under 6,000 pounds it is the manufacturers option to provide one.

4. FCC radio station license if the aircraft is equipped with a radio transmitter.

These items are *required* whether you *own*, *lease*, or *rent* an aircraft!

An aircraft title lists legal ownership of property and specifies any obligations that may be placed against the property. Ideally a "clear title" implies that there are no encumbrances such as liens, chattel mortgages, or other unsatisfied claims against the aircraft. A title search must be conducted to establish the exact title conditions of an aircraft. This may be accomplished a number of different ways. First, you may search the aircraft records yourself. The FAA GADO will be able to assist you in organizing and conducting your search. You may also write to the FAA Aircraft Registry; a list of title search companies AC Form 8050-55 will be furnished upon request. Second, an aircraft title search may be conducted by an attorney or a qualified aircraft title search company. Third, your local banker may be of assistance. Most lending institutions that finance aircraft require a title search before granting a loan. The purchaser of a home wouldn't consider such a transaction without a title search; an aircraft buyer should do no less when purchasing an aircraft.

In general a bill of sale which meets the requirements of FAA Form 8050-2 is adequate to describe aircraft ownership. Other conveyances are a contract of conditional sale, mortgage, assignment of mortgage, or other instruments affecting title to or interest in the property. Part 49 of the FAR's requires that all aircraft titles be recorded. If a person submits a title (a conveyance) for recording and wants the original returned to him, he must submit a true copy with the original. After recording, the copy is kept by the FAA and the original is returned to the applicant stamped with the time and date of recording. The copy must be imprinted on paper permanent in nature, including dates, and signatures to which is attached a certificate by the person submitting the conveyance stating that the copy has been compared with the original and that it is a true copy. If the seller of an aircraft is not shown on the FAA record as

Centerline thrust, an aircraft concept so successful that Cessna Skymaster was adopted by the Air Force as a military observation plane (the 0-2). Featuring no minimum single-engine control speed, the Skymaster has a special FAA Centerline Thrust pilot certificate rating. Cruise speed of the Skymaster is 196 mph.   (Photo courtesy of Cessna Aircraft Co.)

the owner of the aircraft, a conveyance, including a contract of conditional sale, submitted for recording must be accompanied by a bill of sale or similar document showing consecutive transfers from the last registered owner, through each intervening owner, to the seller. Aircraft titles apply to aircraft, engines developing more than 750 horsepower, and propellers able to absorb greater than 750 rated take-off shaft horsepower. The Federal fee for recording an aircraft title is currently $5.00.

If you purchase an aircraft, before you fly it you must apply for a certificate of registration in accordance with FAR 47. An aircraft is eligible for registration only if it is owned by a citizen of the United States, and is not registered under the laws of any foreign country. When applying for a registration certificate, an aircraft bill of sale or other evidence of ownership must be submitted. The certificate of registration does not indicate aircraft ownership as such. The FAA issues a certificate of aircraft registration to the person who appears to be the owner on the basis of the evidence of ownership submitted with the application for aircraft registration, or recorded at the FAA aircraft registry.

To apply for a certificate of aircraft registration it is only necessary to fill out FAA Form 8050-1. The "pink" copy of the application is placed in the aircraft until the permanent certificate of registration is received from the FAA. This certificate, FAA Form 8050-3, replaces the "pink" copy in the aircraft. The certificate of registration expires when:

1. The aircraft is registered under the laws of a foreign country;

2. The registration is cancelled at the written request of the holder of the certificate;

3. The aircraft is totally destroyed or scrapped;

4. Ownership of the aircraft is transferred;

5. The holder of the certificate loses his United States citizenship; or

6. Thirty days have elapsed since the death of the holder of the certificate.

When an aircraft is sold the previous owner (seller) must notify the FAA by filling in the back of his certificate of registration and mailing it to the FAA Aircraft Registry.

The holder of a certificate of aircraft registration is required to submit an Aircraft Registration Eligibility, Identification, and Activity Report. This form must be submitted to the FAA Aircraft

Registry by April 1 each year. Part I is mandatory, Part II is voluntary. Refusal or failure to submit the required information may be cause for suspension or revocation of the holder's certificate of aircraft registration.

Within thirty days after any change in his permanent mailing address, the holder of a certificate of aircraft registration must notify the FAA Aircraft Registry of his new address. A revised certificate of aircraft registration will then be issued without charge.

An aircraft radio station license, FCC Form 556, is a required item of aircraft legal paperwork if the aircraft contains any radio transmitter. Application for an aircraft radio station license (FCC Form 404) may be obtained from your local FCC office or from the Federal Communications Commission, Gettysburg, Pennsylvania, 17325. A new station license is required when the aircraft is first licensed, aircraft ownership is changed, new transmitter equipment is added, or a period of five years has elapsed from original issue (use FCC Form 405-B for renewal, if no change from previous license). The present cost of an aircraft radio station license is $4.00. When an aircraft is sold the seller's radio station license (if valid at the time of sale) remains valid for thirty days for the benefit of the buyer, provided the buyer applies for a new aircraft radio station license at the time of sale.

The FAR's require any owner or operator who sells a U.S. registered aircraft to transfer to the purchaser, at the time of sale the maintenance records of the aircraft. The records must contain at least the following information:

1. The total time in service of the airframe;

2. The current status of life-limited parts of each airframe, engine, propeller, rotor, and appliance;

3. The time since last overhaul of all items installed on the aircraft which are required to be overhauled on a specified time basis;

4. The identification of the current inspection status of the aircraft, including the times since the last inspections required by the inspection program under which the aircraft and its appliances are maintained;

5. The current status of applicable airworthiness directives, including the method of compliance;

6. A list of current major alterations to each airplane, engine, propeller, and appliance.

Maintenance records must contain a description of the work performed, the dates of completion of the work performed, and the signature and certificate number of the person approving the aircraft for return to service. An aircraft owner or operator shall make all maintenance records available to the NTSB if so requested.

In order to fly your new aircraft the FAR's require that a current FAA approved aircraft flight manual*, placards, listings, and instrument markings which describe operating limitations for that aircraft, be available to the pilot. As a minimum, power plant limitations, airspeed operating ranges, aircraft weight and balance limits, minimum flight crew, kinds of operation permitted, and maximum operating altitude must be described.

AIRCRAFT MAINTENANCE

The term "maintenance" applied to an airplane can be subdivided into three categories: inspection, preventive maintenance, repairs and alterations. FAR 91.163 states, "The owner or operator of an aircraft is primarily responsible for maintaining that aircraft in an airworthy condition . . ." Furthermore, FAR 91.165 goes on to state, "each owner or operator of an aircraft shall have the aircraft inspected, etc. . . . In addition, he shall insure that maintenance personnel make appropriate entries in the aircraft and maintenance records indicating the aircraft has been released to service." Thus it becomes very clear that the *aircraft owner or operator* is the *individual responsible* to have the aircraft inspected, preventive maintenance performed, and repairs or alterations made as necessary to maintain the aircraft in an airworthy condition in accordance with its type certificate!

Inspections Required

An airplane must have an annual inspection every twelve calendar months. This inspection may be performed by a certificated airframe and power plant mechanic holding an FAA Inspection Authorization (IA), an FAA certificated repair station, or the manufacturer of the aircraft if he meets the requirements of the regulations. In the event more than twelve calendar months have elapsed from the last annual, the aircraft is no longer airworthy and cannot be flown unless a special FAA ferry permit is obtained.

An aircraft used to carry passengers for hire, or for flight instruction for hire, must be inspected within each 100 hours of time in service by a certificated A & P or IA mechanic, an appropriately rated FAA repair station, or the manufacturer of the aircraft. The annual inspection is acceptable as a 100-hour inspection, but the reverse is not true. The 100-hour limitation may be exceeded by

*If required for that model of aircraft.

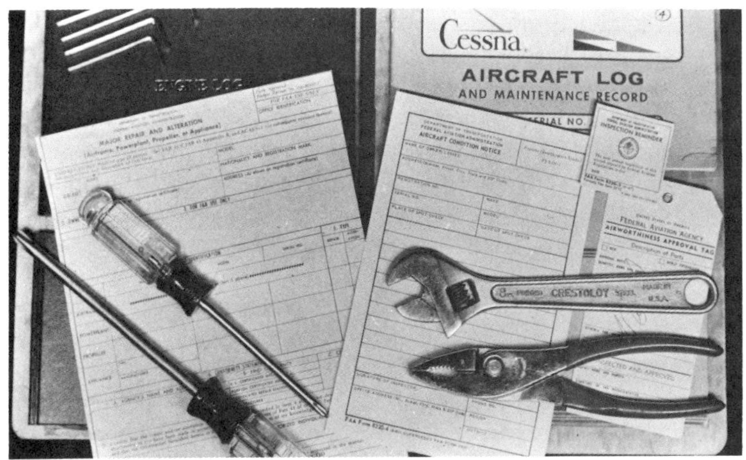

Aircraft maintenance records may at times seem a chore but well kept maintenance logs quickly become a pilot and owner's best friend in the event of an accident, an incident, or sale of an aircraft.

Powered by two 6-cylinder Continental fuel injection engines rated at 285 hp each, the E55 Beech Baron cruises at 230 mph. This sleek aircraft can carry a useful load of over 2,000 lbs. (Photo courtesy of Beech Aircraft Corp.)

not more than 10 hours if necessary to reach a place at which the inspection can be done. The excess time, however, is included in computing the next 100 hours of time in service. When renting an aircraft for a cross-country, take care to check the maintenance records. Assure yourself that adequate time remains to complete your cross-country before the next 100-hour inspection is due. In the event IFR operation is anticipated, additionally check to assure that the altimeter and static system has been inspected within the preceding 24 calendar months.

Following an inspection it is the responsibility of the IA mechanic to certify that the aircraft is again airworthy. This is accomplished by entering in the aircraft maintenance records a description of the type of inspection, the date of the inspection, and the signature and certificate number of the person approving the aircraft for a return to service. In the event an aircraft fails an inspection the IA is obligated to provide a list of discrepancies and unairworthy items to the aircraft owner or lessee. The local FAA district office is similarly provided with a list of discrepancies.

Surprise! The letter from FAA containing form 8320 states that you have been selected to have your aircraft examined for compliance with applicable maintenance standards. Would you kindly grant permission to FAA to conduct an inspection of your aircraft? The use of a "spot check" is a valuable tool in any quality control program and its utilization by FAA is in keeping with a basic responsibility for maintaining standards of aircraft maintenance. Should you be solicited for a spot check of your aircraft, the inspection cost will be borne by FAA and the work will be accomplished at a time convenient to you.

Preventative Maintenance

A significant factor in reducing flying costs is the fact that certain maintenance is not classified as major and thus may be performed by the pilot himself. Federal Aviation Regulations state that "the holder of a pilot certificate issued under FAR 61 may perform preventative maintenance on any aircraft owned or operated by him that is not used in air carrier service." Preventative maintenance means simple or minor preservation operations and the replacement of small standard parts not involving complex assembly operations. Work of the following type is classified as preventative maintenance:

1. Removal, installation, and repair of landing gear tires.

2. Replacing elastic shock absorber cords on landing gear.

3. Servicing landing gear shock struts by adding oil, air, or both.

4. Servicing landing gear wheel bearings, such as cleaning and greasing.

5. Replacing defective safety wiring or cotter keys.

6. Lubrication not requiring disassembly other than removal of nonstructural items such as cover plates, cowlings, and fairings.

7. Making simple fabric patches not requiring rib stitching or the removal of structural parts or control surfaces.

8. Replenishing hydraulic fluid in the hydraulic reservoir.

9. Refinishing decorative coating of fuselage, wings, tail group surfaces (excluding balanced control surfaces), fairings, cowling, landing gear, cabin, or cockpit interior when removal or disassembly of any primary structure or operating system is not required.

10. Applying preservative or protective material to components where no disassembly of any primary structure or operating system is involved and where such coating is not prohibited or is not contrary to good practices.

11. Repairing upholstery and decorative furnishings of the cabin or cockpit interior when the repairing does not require disassembly of any primary structure or operating system or interfere with an operating system or affect primary structure of the aircraft.

12. Making small simple repairs to fairings, nonstructural cover plates, cowlings, and small patches and reinforcements not changing the contour so as to interfere with proper airflow.

13. Replacing side windows where that work does not interfere with the structure or any operating system such as controls, electrical equipment, etc.

14. Replacing safety belts.

15. Replacing seats or seat parts with replacement parts approved for the aircraft, not involving disassembly of any primary structure or operating system.

16. Trouble shooting and repairing broken circuits in landing light wiring circuits.

17. Replacing bulbs, reflectors, and lenses of position and landing lights.

18. Replacing wheels and skis where no weight and balance computation is involved.

19. Replacing any cowling not requiring removal of the propeller or disconnection of flight controls.

20. Replacing or cleaning spark plugs and setting of spark plug gap clearance.

21. Replacing any hose connection except hydraulic connections.

22. Replacing prefabricated fuel lines.

23. Cleaning fuel and oil strainers.

24. Replacing batteries and checking fluid level and specific gravity.

25. Removing and installing glider wings and tail surfaces that are specifically designed for quick removal and installation and when such removal and installation can be accomplished by the pilot.

Major Repairs of Alterations

When a major repair or alteration to an airplane is accomplished, it must be inspected and the airplane returned to service by an A & P mechanic with an FAA Inspection Authorization, or a properly certificated repair station, manufacturer, air carrier or commercial operator. Repair and alteration work may be accomplished by a mechanic, a repair man, *or a person working under the supervision of a mechanic* or repair man *providing* the supervisory mechanic *personally observes* the work being done to the extent necessary to insure that it is accomplished properly. Furthermore, the supervisor must be *readily available, in person,* for consultation during the process. However, the authority to participate in a major repair or alteration does not extend to inspections. Major repairs include such items as the strengthening, reinforcing, splicing, and manufacturing of primary structural members of an aircraft, the overhaul of a power plant, the overhaul of a propeller, and the calibration and repair of instruments and radio equipment. Persons performing a major repair or major alteration are required to describe the service on FAA Form 337; one copy is presented to the aircraft owner and a second copy is forwarded to the local FAA district office.

AIRWORTHINESS DIRECTIVES

Airworthiness directives (commonly referred to as AD's or AD notes), are intended to alert aircraft owners of unsafe aircraft conditions that exist or are likely to exist. The AD note identifies the condition and specifies the required corrective action, and the conditions or limitations, if any, under which the aircraft may continue to be used. FAR's require a chronological record be maintained of all AD's on which action has been taken. This record must include the date, AD number, a brief description of the method of compliance, and the signature and certificate number of the repair station or mechanic who compiled the AD. It is the aircraft owner's responsibility to assure compliance with all pertinent AD's. This includes those AD's that require recurrent or continuing action. For example, an AD may require a certain inspection every 50 flight hours, which means that the particular inspection must be accomplished *and recorded* for every 50 hours of flight.

Airworthiness directives are published in the Federal Register as a formal means of distributing information. In addition, AD's are distributed to certified repair stations and published in summary form in two volumes. Volume I includes directives applicable to small aircraft (12,500 pounds or less); Volume II includes directives applicable to large aircraft. These summaries may be obtained from the Superintendent of Documents, Washington, D.C., by asking for the "Summary of Airworthiness Directives," Vol. I Cat. No. SN 050-007-0036-4 or Vol. II Cat. No. SN 050-007-00307-2. Cost of the summaries is currently $14.00 and $13.00 respectively.

The Airworthiness Directive is one of the finest systems of preventive maintenance yet devised. The rapid distribution of maintenance information throughout the aviation community is in keeping with the basic FAA charter to uphold public safety. AD's are sometimes judgmental in nature and, as such, may be subject to question. However, when equated against the exorbitant cost of funerals even the most questionable AD is still a bargain. AD's are issued by the FAA based upon recommendations of the NTSB, recommendations of manufacturers, or as a result of accident statistics.

CHAPTER 4
PREFLIGHT PLANNING

RESPONSIBILITY AND AUTHORITY OF THE PILOT-IN-COMMAND

Aviation regulations are sometimes short in their narrative form and at the same time extensive in coverage. The regulations which define the responsibility and authority of the Pilot-in-Command (PIC) are of this exact nature; brief, concise, and far-reaching in meaning and intent.

FAR 91.3 states: *"The pilot-in-command of an aircraft is directly responsible for, and is the final authority as to, the operation of that aircraft."* This brief but important regulation defines without doubt that the pilot-in-command is the individual responsible for the operation and safety of the aircraft. Just who is the pilot-in-command?

1. Student Pilot: A student pilot is the pilot-in-command during all authorized solo flights of his training and during the flight test as an applicant for a pilot certificate.

2. Private and Commercial Pilots: A private, commercial, or air transport pilot is considered pilot-in-command during such time he (or she) is the sole manipulator of the controls of an aircraft for which he is rated, or when the sole occupant of an aircraft, or when acting as pilot-in-command of an aircraft on which more than one pilot is required under the type certification for the aircraft.

3. Flight Instructors: A certificated flight instructor is the pilot-in-command during all flight time in which he acts in the capacity of a flight instructor.

4. Flight Examiners: FAA inspectors or other authorized flight examiners are *not* pilot-in-command of an aircraft during a flight test unless required to act in that capacity for the flight, or a portion of the flight. Basically, the inspector observes the applicants ability to perform procedures and maneuvers of the flight test.

5. All Pilots: To act as pilot-in-command one must have a valid pilot certificate for the type of aircraft involved, possess a current medical certificate, and meet recency of flight experience requirements.

When a pilot elects to act as pilot-in-command, the authority granted by this position carries with it the undeniable responsibilities of the post.

PREFLIGHT RESPONSIBILITY OF THE PILOT-IN-COMMAND

FAR 91.5 states: *"Each pilot-in-command, shall before beginning a flight, familiarize himself with all available information concerning that flight."* As an absolute minimum this information must include weather reports and forecasts, fuel requirements, and alternate landing fields for flights extending a distance greater than 25 statute miles from the departure airport. In addition, the pilot-in-command must familiarize himself with runway lengths at airports of intended use as well as take-off and landing distances taking into account airport elevation, runway slope, aircraft gross weight, wind conditions, temperature and density altitude. As the person responsible for, and final authority as to the operation of an aircraft, the pilot-in-command is also obligated to determine that the aircraft is airworthy prior to flight.

Route Planning

The requirement that a pilot-in-command "familiarize himself with *all available information* concerning that flight . . .", demands careful attention to planning the flight route and possible alternates. As a minimum the following items are suggested:

1. Obtain current Sectional or World Aeronautical Charts which cover the intended route of flight and alternates or route deviations that may be required. Review the intended route of flight for obstacles; don't be surprised to see hazards such as 1000 feet high TV antennas directly on airways or in the very near vicinity of airports! Using the distances involved make a preliminary (no wind) estimate of the fuel required to accomplish the flight. Plan at least a 45 minute fuel reserve. Prior to departure upgrade the estimate using forecast winds aloft information. Compute required compass headings. Although

modern navigation is conducted basically by the use of radio aids, the process of dead reckoning is a valuable back-up.

2. Review thoroughly all radio aids available on the intended route of flight including alternate routes or destinations. This information is available in brief on sectional charts. However, a more thorough source of information is the Airman's Information Manual Part 3, Operational Data and Notices to Airmen. This reference contains an airport-facility directory of all major airports with control towers, a tabulation of radio navigation aids and frequencies, information for updating sectional charts, general and special notices to airmen, a list of new and permanently closed airports, an index of military training routes (heavy wagon and oil burner routes), and an index of special operations such as Terminal Control Areas or recommended VFR flight routes. Part 3 of the AIM may be obtained on an annual subscription basis from the Superintendent of Documents, Government Printing Office, Washington, D.C., 20402, at a current cost of 22 dollars per year. Part 3 as well as all other parts of the AIM are available for use *free of charge* by either telephoning or visiting your local Flight Service Station.

3. If your flight includes airports which are not major airports, Part 2, the Airport Directory, should be consulted. Part 2 contains a directory of *all* airports, seaplane bases, and heliports available for civil use. Part 2 also contains a listing of airports of entry, a listing of Flight Service Stations, and Weather Bureau telephone numbers. This part of the AIM is issued semi-annually at a current cost of $7.00 per year.

4. To obtain information on VOR receiver check points or VOR restrictions (such as shadowing due to mountains) it is necessary to consult Part 4, Graphic Notices and Supplemental Data. This part of the AIM contains a listing of VOR check points, restrictions to on-route navigational aids, a tabulation of parachute jump areas, and special notices of interest to airmen. Part 4, issued semi-annually, is available on an annual subscription basis at a current cost of $9.50 per year.

5. It is required by FAR that each pilot-in-command determine the runway length(s) at airports of intended use as well as calculate the expected take-off and landing distance based upon the density altitude and aircraft performance characteristics. Unfortunately, the AIM and sectional charts list only the length of the longest runway. Complete airport information, however, is available in several commercial publications. The JEPPESEN AIRWAY MANUAL as used for IFR flight is an extensive source of airport information. This manual is generally available at most fixed based operators. A second source is AIRPORT DIAGRAMS, published by Sporty's Pilot Shop, Batavia, Ohio, 45103

As a family airplane, the Cessna Skyhawk is hard to beat. With a cruise speed of 132 mph, an economical 150 hp engine, and a roomy four person capacity it's easy to understand why the Skyhawk/172 is the world's best selling airplane.

(Photo courtesy of Cessna Aircraft Co.)

A new member of the Piper family, the Cherokee Challenger cruises at 141 mph using a 180 hp Lycoming for power. This aircraft will carry a useful load of 1,064 lbs.

(Photo courtesy of Piper Aircraft Corp.)

Computing take-off distance and rate of climb? Naturally your aircraft flight manual is a desired source. However, a handy aid for this purpose is the Denalt Performance Computer illustrated in the accompanying figure. These computers are for sale by the Superintendent of Documents, U.S. Government Printing Office, Washington, D.C., 20402, at a current price of 50¢ each. Be sure and specify whether you want a computer for a fixed pitch propeller aircraft or a constant speed propeller aircraft.

6. If your flight route contains segments which are off established airways or into wilderness areas, consider carrying an appropriate survival kit. For night flight at least one flashlight is an absolute must.

7. Make sure your airplane isn't due an annual inspection (or a 100 hour inspection in the case of a rented aircraft). Remember, it's up to the pilot-in-command to determine the airworthiness of the aircraft.

8. Now check the weight and balance of your aircraft. Both items *must* be within the manufacturers allowable limits.

WEATHER BRIEFING

The weather briefing is perhaps the single most important item to be accomplished as a part of preflight planning. Aviation weather information is available 24 hours-a-day, seven-days-a-week, with distribution via radio, telephone, or by person-to-person briefing at your local FSS. Of these means for obtaining a weather briefing, the person-to-person review with a flight service specialist is by far the preferred method. To obtain a briefing suited to your needs, advise the weather briefer of your qualifications as a pilot (student, private, instrument-rated or not), time and place of departure, type aircraft; N number of aircraft, proposed route of flight, destination, and estimated time of arrival. This will advise the briefer of the type and extent of weather information required. As a minimum determine the following:

1. Expected weather at departure airport at time of departure.

2. Forecast weather on route.

3. Forecast weather at destination airport.

4. Locations and movement of major weather systems such as fronts, areas of precipitation, thunderstorms, icing, fog, turbulence, etc.

5. In the event weather along your intended route is marginal,

plan an alternate route or destination and obtain a weather briefing accordingly. Uncertain VFR weather at a destination airport may necessitate an extra fuel stop as a precautionary move. Whatever the case plan "a way out" *before* flight departure.

6. Write down the pertinent facts of your weather briefing.

A Flight Log

Cross-country flight planning requires reference to a number of charts, books, manuals, the weather briefer, and a flight computer. The pay-off resulting from good flight planning is that the library of information consulted to perform the planning process *need not* be taken in the aircraft. The results of proper flight planning can be entered on a single sheet of paper not much larger than the size of a page of this book. The associated figure illustrates a typical flight plan and enroute flight log. Good flight planning results in the following minimal material being carried during flight:

1. Sectional or Wac Charts of the flight route.
2. A flight computer and plotter.
3. A flight planning log (sheet of paper No. 1), and
4. A weather briefing log (sheet of paper No. 2).

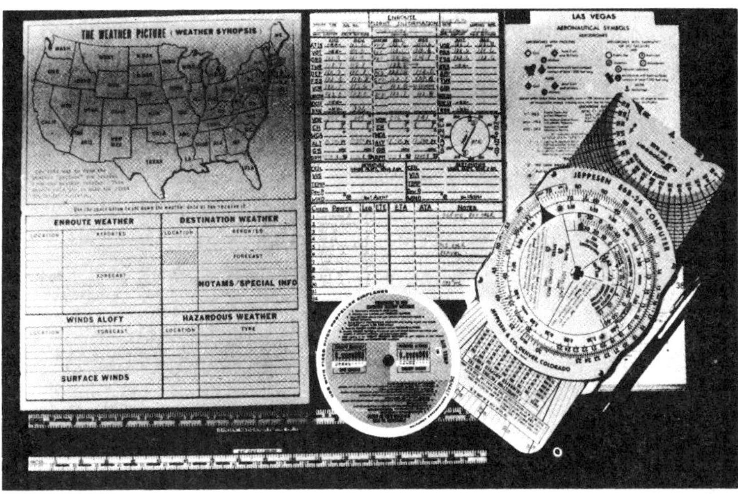

Flying doesn't require an aviation library be carried aloft. A weather briefing record, flight log, map (current issue), computer, and plotter will do for VFR flight. A Denalt Computer is convenient for calculating take-off and rate of climb performance.

Filing A Flight Plan

Every pilot is urged to file a flight plan prior to departure. Although not required by regulation (for VFR flight operation) the flight plan is the best form of term insurance any pilot could take and the cost is absolutely zero. For those VFR pilots who elect to use this service, FAR 91 lists the information required on the flight plan. For the most part the information is self-evident. However, certain of the blocks (see figure) deserve additional explanation. Block 1 is checked for VFR flight with Block 2 the N number of the aircraft. Block 3 is for specifying the type of aircraft including any special equipment carried. Although listing of transponder/DME equipment is only required for IFR flight plans, it is an excellent VFR practice. The following code table applies:

SPECIAL EQUIPMENT CODES

```
/X   Transponder, no code
/T   Transponder, with 64 code capability
/U   Transponder, with 4096 code capability
/D   DME
/L   DME and transponder, no code
/B   DME and transponder, with 64 code
     capability
/A   DME and transponder, with 4096 code
     capability
/C   No code transponder and approved
     area navigation
/F   4096 code transponder and approved
     area navigation
/S   64 code transponder and approved
     area navigation
/W   No transponder and approved area
     navigation
```

Block 4 is the true air speed of the aircraft in knots and Block 5 is the point of departure. Block 6 is used to denote the proposed Zulu departure time. Upon opening your flight plan (by radio), flight service will fill in your actual Zulu departure time. Block 7 provides for a record of your proposed MSL Altitude on the initial leg of your flight. Particular attention should be given to Block 8 to describe an accurate record of your flight route. Block 9 is self-evident. Block 10 is a *total* time estimate beginning at the estimated time of departure and ending at the estimated time of arrival including ground time spent enroute for purposes of refueling, etc. Block 11 provides the pilot an opportunity to list special conditions pertain-

FLIGHT PLAN RECORD (FAA Use Only)

1. TYPE	2. AIRCRAFT IDENTIFICATION	3. AIRCRAFT TYPE/ SPECIAL EQUIPMENT	4. TRUE AIRSPEED	5. DEPARTURE POINT	6. DEPARTURE TIME		7. CRUISING ALTITUDE
☒ VFR / IFR / DVFR	N1135Y	CESSNA 150/U	100 KTS	PHX	PROPOSED (Z) 1500	ACTUAL (Z)	10,500

8. ROUTE OF FLIGHT

V257, BCE

9. DESTINATION (Name of airport and city)	10. EST. TIME EN ROUTE		11. REMARKS
BRYCE CANYON	HOURS 3	MINUTES 35	REFUEL @ GCN, 20 MIN. 121.5/243 ELT ON BOARD

12. FUEL ON BOARD		13. ALTERNATE AIRPORT(S)	14. PILOT'S NAME, ADDRESS, TELEPHONE NUMBER, AND AIRCRAFT HOME BASE	15. NUMBER ABOARD
HOURS 4	MINUTES 00		J. J. JONES 999-9999 1234 SUNSET, PHX. ARZ SKYHARBOR, TIEDOWN 999	2

16. COLOR OF AIRCRAFT		SPECIALIST INITIALS	TIME STARTED	
ORG/WHT	☒ WEATHER BRIEFING			☐ VNR

FAA Form 7233—3 (3–72)   GPO: 1972 OF—462–477

This simple flight plan record form is all that needs to be filled out to insure the services of FSS and Air Rescue should an emergency arise.

ing to his flight. Typical examples are:

1. Refueling at ________________ airport.

2. Touch and go practice landings will be made at ________________ airport enroute.

3. 121.5/243 Mhz emergency locater beacon on board.

4. VIP on board.

5. Student cross-country, solo.

6. Radio inoperative.

7. 90 channel radio.

8. Ambulatory case aboard.

9. Will avoid all restricted areas.

10. Advise customs of arrival.

Block 12 is self-evident. Block 13 is for listing alternate airports and is used primarily for IFR flights. Block 14 is to list the full name of the pilot-in-command, home address, telephone number, and aircraft home base (including tie-down number). Should no one be present at the listed address (as in the case of a family vacation) it is desirable that Block 14 contain the name, address, and telephone number of a friend or a relative who would be familiar with the pilot. Blocks 15 and 16 are self-evident. The remaining Blocks are for use by flight service personnel. However, special attention should be directed to the letters VNR in the lower right hand block. These stand for Visual flight Not Recommended! This formally records the fact that a flight service specialist advised against a VFR flight!

After a flight plan has been filed and opened, the pilot-in-command is responsible to notify the nearest FAA Flight Service Station to close the flight plan upon completion of his flight. VFR flight plans are closed only by FSS, not by tower or radar as for an IFR flight plan. In the event a pilot fails to close his flight plan the following actions are initiated by FSS:

1. Thirty minutes after ETA: FSS initiates a radio telephone communication search of all airports along the proposed flight route and in the local area of the destination airport listed on the flight plan. (In some instances a local area includes as many as 50 airports). The radio telephone communication search also includes contact with local law enforcement agencies.

2. One and one-half hours after ETA: An Alert Notice is issued. The result is an extended communications search for information throughout the area within flight range of the aircraft. Search assistance is requested from flights traversing the search area.

3. Two and one-half hours after ETA: Search and rescue is notified of a missing aircraft; appropriate civilian air patrol and military search action is initiated.

The procedure for closing a flight plan is not difficult since a Flight Service Station is as close as the aircraft radio or a telephone. Attention to this simple matter at the destination of a flight enables search and rescue procedures to be utilized for the purpose for which they were developed—to help the pilot in distress.

Aircraft Instruments and Equipment Required For VFR Flight

As a part of the preflight process it is necessary that the pilot-in-command examine his aircraft to assure conformance with FAR's which describe instruments and equipment required. For VFR flights during the day in a standard category aircraft the following instruments and equipment are required:

1. Airspeed indicator

2. Altimeter

3. Compass

4. Tachometer

5. Oil pressure gauge (one for each engine).

The Cessna Cardinal RG is without doubt one of today's most beautifully styled aircraft. Using a 200 hp engine, this aircraft will carry a 1,140 lb. useful load at a cruise speed of 171 mph for some 945 miles.   (Photo courtesy of Cessna Aircraft Co.)

The Cessna Cardinal RG instrument panel meets FAA requirements for VFR and IFR flight (compass not shown).
(Photo courtesy of Cessna Aircraft Co.)

6. Temperature gauge (one for each liquid-cooled engine).

7. Oil Temperature gauge (one for each air-cooled engine).

8. Manifold pressure gauge (one for each engine). This instrument is required for engines which are supercharged or aircraft which have been certified with a manifold pressure gauge.

9. Fuel gauge(s) (as required to indicate the quantity of fuel in each tank).

10. Landing gear position indicator (retractable aircraft only).

11. Approved flotation gear for each occupant and at least one pyrotechnic signaling device if the aircraft is to be operated for hire over water and beyond power-off gliding distance from shore. This applies to any aircraft regardless of the number of engines.

12. Safety belts for all occupants who have reached their second birthday.

If VFR flight is to be conducted at night the following are additionally required:

1. A red left and green right wing light and a white tail light.

2. A red or white anti-collision light (rotating beacon or strobe).

3. Electric landing light (if the aircraft is operated for hire).

4. A generator whose capacity is adequate to power all electrical and radio equipment required to conduct the flight.

5. One spare set of fuses, or three spare fuses of each kind required.

For flight involving aerobatics or unusual attitudes each occupant of the aircraft must wear an approved parachute. (Unusual attitudes are defined as bank angles exceeding 60 degrees relative to the horizon and pitch angles exceeding 30 degrees): If a chair type parachute is employed, it must have been packed by an appropriately rated parachute rigger within the preceding 120 days. If other types of parachutes are employed, such must have been packed by an appropriately rated rigger within the preceding 60 days.

Flights to be made at high altitudes require additional planning as to oxygen for the pilot and passengers. Federal Aviation Regulations require that oxygen be provided the flight crew for all aircraft operating at cabin pressure altitudes of 12,500 feet MSL up to and including 14,000 feet MSL for any part of the flight of more than 30 minutes duration at these altitudes. Above 14,000 feet MSL, the flight crew is required to use supplemental oxygen during the entire time at these altitudes; and, above 15,000 feet MSL, each occupant of the aircraft must be provided supplemental oxygen.

In reality, the altitude limits for supplemental oxygen as prescribed by FAR are quite liberal. Studies indicate that all persons begin to deteriorate in alertness and mental efficiency to some degree above 12,000 feet without supplemental oxygen. Above 14,000 feet distinct impairment of mental facilities occurs—especially with respect to mathematical reasoning capabilities. Night vision is sharply impaired at higher altitudes, even though other symptoms of hypoxia may not be apparent. It is said that a pilot flying at night without supplemental oxygen is 24% blind at 8,000 feet and 50% blind at 12,000 feet. Individual physical fitness and other factors may change a person's tolerance to hypoxia. Smoking at 10,000 feet produces effects equivalent to those experienced at 14,000 feet without smoking.

Recent congressional legislation has established the requirement that all aircraft be equipped with an Emergency Locater ransmitter (ELT) before December 30, 1973 (newly manufactured civil aircraft must be so equipped after December 30, 1971). For civil usage emergency locater transmitters may be of either the fixed or deployable types; units must be attached to the airplane in a manner that the probability of damage to the transmitter is minimized in the event of a crash impact. Batteries used in the emergency locater transmitters must be replaced when (a) the transmitter has been in use for more than one cumulative hour or, (b) when 50% of the useful life of the batteries has expired (per mfgr. ratings). Exceptions to the requirements for an emergency locater transmitter apply in cases of ferrying an aircraft for the installation or repair of an emergency locater transmitter, training flights conducted within a 20-mile radius of the airport from which the flight began, or in the case of agricultural aircraft operations. Older model emergency locater transmitter equipment may be utilized until December 30, 1975 provided (a) the installation was approved before October 21, 1971, (b) the device transmits simultaneously on 121.5 and 243.0 Mhz., (c) the device was manufactured under TSO-C61a, and (d) the emergency locater transmitter is attached to the airplane and is in operable condition.

Preflight preparations are not complete until a thorough check of the adequacy and operability of all necessary radio equipment has been made by the pilot-in-command. A communications transmitter-receiver is required for flight into fields where traffic is controlled by a tower. Similarly a 4,096 code transponder is required for operation in Group I Terminal Control Areas. A check on the operability of your communications transmitter-receiver can be accomplished by calling ground control, FSS, or Unicom prior to taxi. A request for a "radio check" will bring a reply of the signal strength and modulation quality of your transmitter. Navigational receiver equipment may be checked in many cases prior to flight by tuning to the Very High Frequency Omni Test signal (VOT) provided at many major airports. Part 3 of the AIM lists airports so equipped and the frequency for use. As an alternate technique, Part 4 of the AIM lists VOR receiver check points that may be used at airports not equipped with a VOT. Although formal VOR receiver accuracy limits are not specified for VFR flight, the FAR requirements for IFR receiver accuracy provide an excellent guide. These requirements are ±4 degrees for a ground VOR receiver check and ±6 degrees for an airborn VOR receiver check. Transponder equipment may be checked prior to flight by utilizing the self-test feature or far better by requesting a "transponder check" from ATC (line of sight conditions permitting).

The Final Step

The final step in the process of preflight planning is an aircraft examination and engine run-up. Assuming that the engine(s) and propeller(s) operate in accordance with the manufacturer's run-up specifications and the associated instruments operate properly, the aircraft preflight is complete. Now let's set the altimeter to the field altitude and check the barometric pressure shown in the Kollsman window with the altimeter setting. An error greater than ±1″ Hg (100 feet) indicates a need for altimeter servicing.

Federal aircraft regulations require that the pilot keep his seat belt fastened during all phases of flight. Each person on board an aircraft must occupy a seat with a safety belt properly secured about him. However, a child who has not reached his second birthday may be held by an adult. In the event the purpose of the flight is for sport parachuting, parachutists on board may use the floor of the aircraft as a seat. As pilot-in-command it is your responsibility to advise passengers to fasten their seat belts prior to take-off or landing and in the event of anticipated and actual turbulence conditions.

The pilot-in-command is the individual responsible for *all phases of safety* during both aircraft ground and flight operations. He accomplishes the necessary preflight planning, inspects the aircraft as required to determine its airworthiness, and is considerate of passenger safety from boarding to exit at the destination airport.

CHAPTER 5
THE AIRSPACE

Part I
Subdivisions of the Airspace

Airspace needs of the pilot, the air traveller, and the community are many and varied. Airspace restrictions result for reasons of safety and equality in sharing a national resource. In certain instances the density of aircraft movements necessitates the airspace be subdivided into carefully defined regions with special operating procedures. In other instances special use airspace is reserved for training of military personnel, testing of missiles, etc. Due to the many and varied airspace needs a number of different airspace subdivisions result. The first part of this chapter is devoted to definitions of the various airspace subdivisions and the second part to general flight operations within our national airspace.

DISTRIBUTION OF THE NATIONAL AIRSPACE

The national airspace system can be diagrammed as shown in the figure on the following page. As illustrated the national airspace is divided into the two major categories, controlled and uncontrolled airspace. Since uncontrolled airspace represents a minimal regulation condition there are no sub-categories in the classification. Controlled airspace, on the other hand, is subdivided into a number of basic and special use types of airspace. East of the Mississippi River about 70% of the airspace is controlled; in the West, about 25%, and along the West Coast, about 70%. A third subdivision is voluntary flight procedure airspace. Typically volunteer flight procedure airspace is located over national parks or major cities. Pilots are requested to fly at altitudes greater than the minimum FAR limit for ecology and noise abatement reasons. Adherence to voluntary flight procedures is highly desirable as a means of preventing our already complex airspace from becoming even more difficult.

Visibility Considerations

The two major divisions of the National Airspace System, controlled and uncontrolled, segregate regions of sparse air traffic from blocks of airspace that support large volumes of flight operations. The word "control" *does not* imply operation with an ATC ground facility (except for IFR flight and certain special VFR cases). In reality the word control denotes minimum acceptable visibility criteria for flight while in controlled airspace. As VFR flight is based on the "see and be seen" principle, cockpit visibility must be adequate for the pilot to detect and avoid conflicting traffic as well as ground obstacles. Thus it is logical that minimum limits for visibility, cloud clearance, and ceiling be established; limits which are consistent with the "see and avoid" concept.

FAR 91.105 provides basic VFR visibility, cloud clearance, and ceiling limits for flight in both uncontrolled and controlled airspace. These limits are illustrated in the accompanying table.

VISUAL FLIGHT RULES

Altitude	Flight visibility	Distance from clouds
1,200 feet or less above the surface (regardless of MSL altitude)—		
Within controlled airspace __________	3 statute miles ________	500 feet below. 1,000 feet above. 2,000 feet horizontal.
Outside controlled airspace __________	1 statute mile except for helicopters	Clear of clouds.
More than 1,200 feet above the surface but less than 10,000 feet MSL—		
Within controlled airspace __________	3 statute miles ________	500 feet below. 1,000 feet above. 2,000 feet horizontal.
Outside controlled airspace __________	1 statue mile _________	500 feet below. 1,000 feet above. 2,000 feet horizontal.
More than 1,200 feet above the surface and at or above 10,000 feet MSL.	5 statute miles ________	1,000 feet below. 1,000 feet above. 1 mile horizontal.

It will be noticed that when operating above 10,000 feet MSL, the visibility and cloud clearance limits are the same for controlled and uncontrolled airspace. In the zone from 1,200 feet Above Ground Level (AGL) to 10,000 feet Mean Sea Level (MSL) the only difference between controlled and uncontrolled airspace is a visibility requirement of three miles when in controlled airspace and one mile in uncontrolled airspace. For operations from the surface level to 1,200 feet AGL in uncontrolled airspace flight requirements are simply one mile visibility and clear of the clouds. However, for operating in the same altitude region in controlled

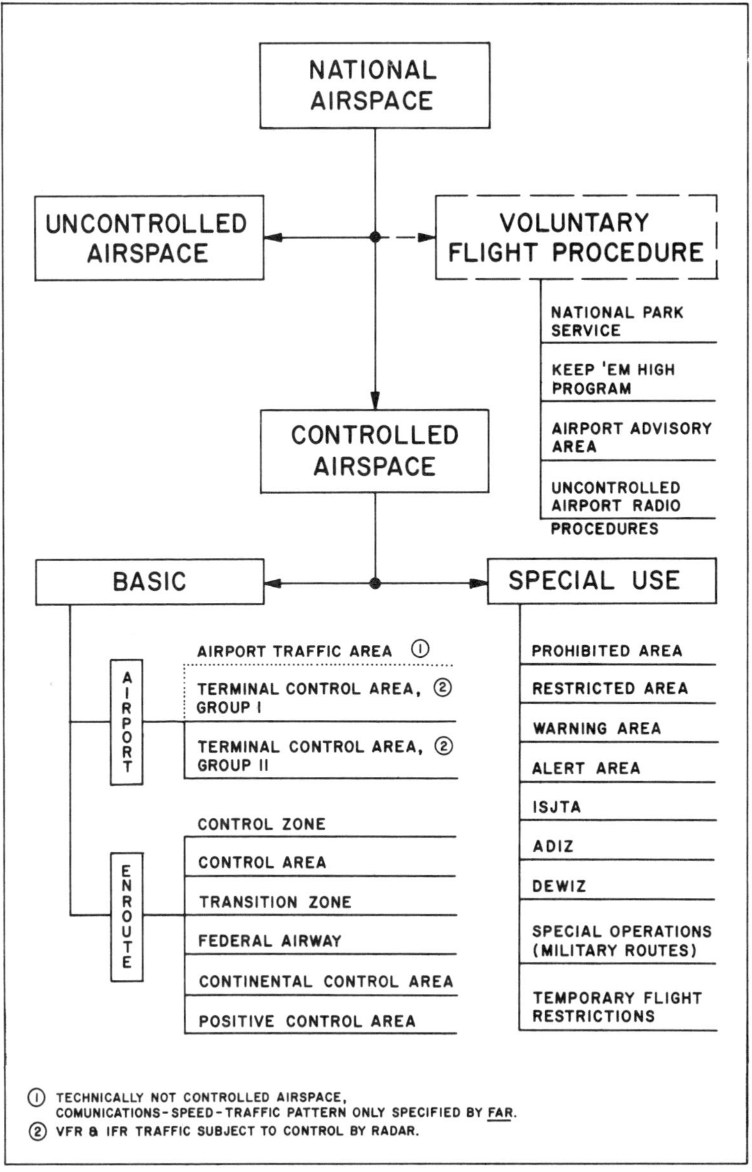

Our National Airspace is divided into various major and minor categories depending upon the use and/or aerial activity involved.

For true VFR flying, how can one beat the Evans VP-1 Volks-plane! Powered by a Volkswagon engine, the VP-1 is all wood construction, weighs 440 lbs., and will cruise at 75 mph. Plans are available from Evans Aircraft Co., Box 744, La Jolla, California 92037.

(Photo courtesy of Evans Aircraft Co.)

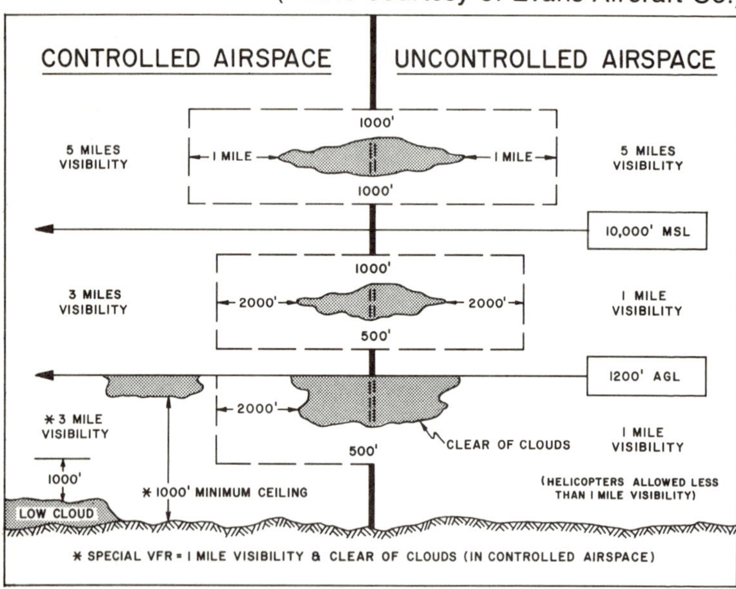

The primary difference between controlled and uncontrolled airspace is a requirement for greater visibility and cloud clearance limits in controlled airspace (below 10,000' MSL).

airspace, the minimum allowable visibility is three miles, a minimum ceiling of 1,000 feet, and a cloud clearance of 2,000 feet horizontally, 500 feet below, and 1,000 feet above. Should weather conditions exist that make visibility, ceiling or cloud clearance limits less than indicated by the accompanying table, VFR flight cannot be conducted; IFR conditions prevail. The single exception to this regulation is special VFR. In this instance certain airports are permitted to authorize an aircraft to enter a controlled area when conditions are less than three miles visibility and/or 1,000 feet ceiling. Under special VFR the minimums are reduced to one mile visibility and clear of the clouds.

"Blocks" of Airspace

The study of our National Airspace is simplified by first considering "blocks" of airspace on an individual basis. For this reason the remainder of this section is an "airspace outline"; an outline that briefly defines each block of airspace including a digest of FAR's pertaining to flight within the particular block.

I. Uncontrolled Airspace.

Airspace in which minimal VFR visibility and cloud restrictions apply. Airspace of this nature is generally located in remote areas and extends in altitude from the surface nominally to 14,500 feet MSL (floor of the Continental Control Area). Often the ceiling of uncontrolled airspace is limited to 700 or 1,200 feet AGL by an overlaying transition area or control area. Aerobatics are permitted in uncontrolled airspace.

II. "Controlled Procedure" Airspace.

The following two common airspace allocations are characterized by various FAR procedures but are technically uncontrolled airspace from the standpoint of ceiling and visibility limits.

1. Airport Traffic Area.

The airspace within a horizontal radius of 5 statute miles from the geographical center of any airport at which a control tower *is operating,* extending from the surface of the airport up to an altitude of 3,000 feet above the elevation of the airport. Within an airport traffic area the following regulations apply:

a. Flight operations are intended for purposes of takeoff and landing only. Should it be desirable to penetrate an airport traffic area (perhaps due to a low ceiling), it is necessary to obtain an ATC clearance from the tower before entering the area (initial call-up should be made 15 miles out). Two-way communications with the tower are required while in an airport traffic area (unless landing at a non-tower airport within an airport traffic area of another airport).

b. Turbine powered aircraft shall maintain a traffic pattern altitude of at least 1,500 feet above the surface when operating to an airport within an airport traffic area. A recommended* traffic pattern altitude for other aircraft is 1,000 feet if the airport is located in a control zone; 800 feet for an airport located in uncontrolled airspace. If a 1,000 foot ceiling were to exist, the traffic pattern altitude in controlled airspace would become 500 feet (minimum cloud clearance) but would remain 800 feet in uncontrolled airspace (clear of clouds).

c. The traffic pattern shall be flown as a lefthand pattern unless noted otherwise by a segmented circle, instructions from tower, a flashing amber light, or as listed in the AIM.

d. Speed limits within an airport traffic area are: Reciprocating engine aircraft: 156 knots (180 MPH) Turbine powered aircraft: 200 knots (230 MPH). If located within a TCA the speed limit is 250 knots (288 MPH).

e. Departure routing shall comply with procedures established for that airport; turbine powered airplanes and large aircraft shall climb to an altitude of 1,500 feet above the surface as rapidly as practicable.

f. At an airport with an operating control tower no pilot may taxi an aircraft on a runway, or takeoff, or land an aircraft unless he has received a clearance from ATC. A clearance to "taxi to" a runway is a clearance to cross all intersecting runways but is not a clearance to "taxi on" the assigned runway.

g. In the event of an aircraft radio failure in flight a pilot may continue to operate the aircraft and land at a tower controlled airport if weather conditions are at or above VFR weather minimums. He must

*Except for special cases, FAR's do not specify traffic pattern altitudes; the values noted are conventions in use.

maintain visual contact with tower and adhere to the following light signals as a means of communications:

LIGHT SIGNALS

Color and Type of Signal	On the Ground	In Flight
STEADY GREEN	Cleared for take-off	Cleared to land
FLASHING GREEN	Cleared to taxi	Return for landing (to be followed by steady green at proper time)
STEADY RED	Stop	Give way to other aircraft and continue circling
FLASHING RED	Taxi clear of landing area (runway) in use	Airport unsafe—do not land
FLASHING WHITE	Return to starting point on airport	
ALTERNATING RED & GREEN	General Warning Signal—Exercise Extreme Caution	

h. The dimensions of an airport traffic area are not shown on sectional maps. The letters CT in the airport data description block indicate that an airport traffic area is located at that airport.

2. Airport Advisory Area.

The area within five statute miles of an airport where a control tower is not operating but where a Flight Service Station is located (a ceiling limit is not specified). At such locations the FSS provides advisory service to arriving and departing aircraft. The following regulations apply:

a. Arriving aircraft shall make all traffic pattern turns to the left unless the airport displays light signals or visual markings indicating that turns should be made to the right.

b. Departing aircraft shall comply with FAA traffic patterns for that airport.

Although it is not mandatory that pilots participate in the airport advisory service program it is strongly recommended that they do so. The following procedure is suggested:

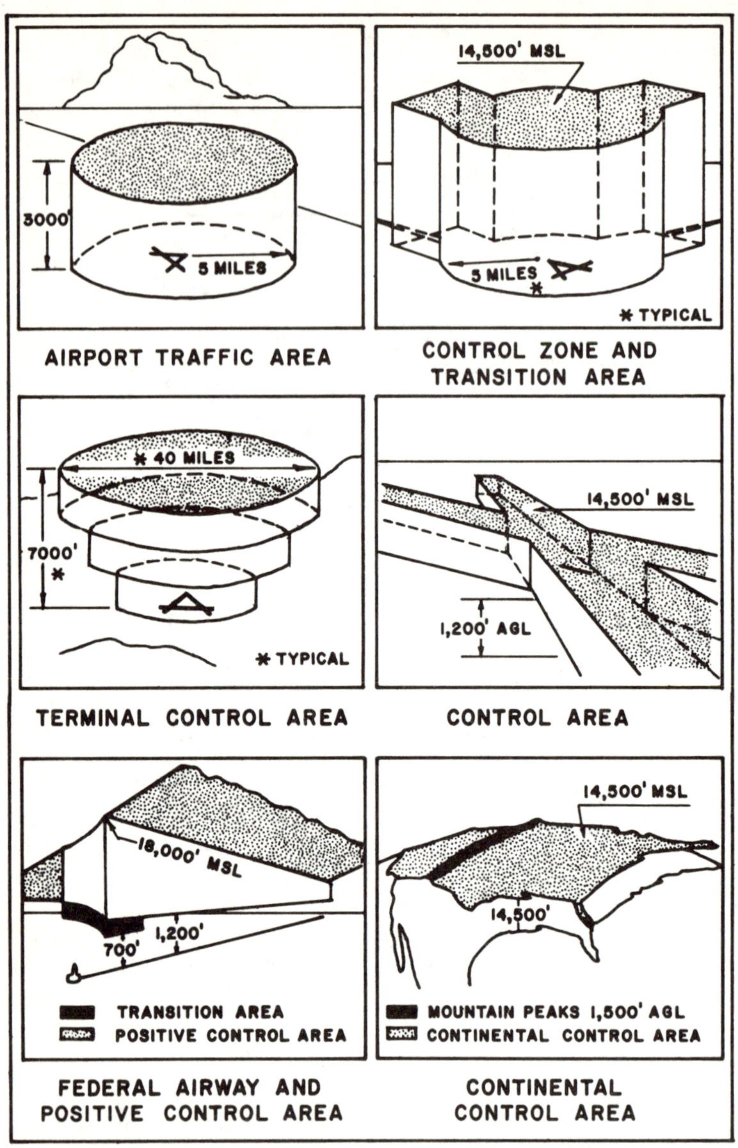

Controlled airspace comes in a variety of sizes and shapes. Except for the airport traffic area, the above figures illustrate basic controlled airspace configurations. The airport traffic area is technically not controlled airspace; FAR's apply only to communications, speed limits, and landing/takeoff procedures. Visibility and cloud clearance limits in an airport traffic area are the same as for uncontrolled airspace (unless the airport traffic area is located in a control zone).

88

c. Arriving aircraft operating VFR contact FSS 15 miles from the airport; advise position, altitude, and intentions. Continue to advise FSS of position entering downwind, base, final, and clear of the active runway.

d. Departing aircraft contact FSS for pre-taxi advisories. Advise FSS when clear of the active runway and leaving the airport advisory area.

The same procedure is useful at airports where there is neither a control tower or FSS. In such instances the Unicom frequency 122.8 Mhz. should be used to advise the local airport operator as well as other possible air traffic.

III. Controlled Airspace.

Airspace in which increased visibility, ceiling, and cloud clearance limits generally apply is termed controlled airspace; additional restrictions may also apply depending upon the reason for control.

1. Control Zone

Airspace which extends upward from the surface nominally to 14,500 feet (the base of the Continental Control Area). In general, control zones are located about airports and are normally circular in shape with a radius of five statute miles plus extensions as necessary for instrument departure and arrival paths. A control zone may encompass more than one airport. Control zones are depicted on charts by a dotted blue line.

2. Control Areas and Federal Airways

Control areas consist of all federal airways plus airspace areas needed to interconnect the federal airway system. A federal airway is eight nautical miles in width and typically extends from 1,200 feet AGL to 18,000 feet MSL. Sectional maps use a shaded blue outline to denote control area floors of 1,200 feet above the surface. Control area floors other than 1,200 feet above the surface are noted with an appropriate numerical value.

3. Transition Area

Controlled airspace which extends upward generally from 700 feet or more above the surface to the floor of the overlying controlled airspace. The basic function of the transition area is to provide a zone of controlled airspace for IFR operations in process of descent or climb while in the near vicinity of an airport. Transition zones are noted by a magenta colored outline on sectional maps.

4. Continental Control Area

   The continental control area consists of the airspace above the United States and Alaska (excluding the Alaska Peninsula) at and above 14,500 feet MSL but does not include the airspace less than 1,500 feet above the surface of the earth or certain prohibited or restricted areas. For all practical purposes, the continental control area may be thought of as a large blanket covering the United States and Alaska with provisions for a 1,500-foot clearance where it passes over mountainous regions. The ceiling of the continental control area is infinity.

5. Positive Control Area

   Airspace so designated that flight must be conducted *only under instrument flight rules*. For operations within positive control areas, aircraft must be:

   a. Equipped with instruments and equipment for IFR operation and flown by a pilot rated and current for instrument flight.

   b. Equipped with a coded radar beacon transponder.

   c. Equipped with communications radio transmitter-receiver equipment necessary to the flight.

   d. Equipped with Distance Measuring Equipment (DME) if the operation is above flight level 240. Positive control area exists from 18,000 feet MSL to flight level 600 throughout the United States.

6. Terminal Control Area (TCA)

   Terminal Control areas are in reality "super air traffic control areas" where *all aircraft* are subject to direction by ATC. Terminal control areas vary in shape in that they are designed to accommodate the particular airport they service. In general, they extend from the surface level to an altitude of 7,000 feet MSL. Group I terminal control areas are located at the busiest airports in the United States with Group II terminal control areas at less congested locations. The following regulations apply to Group I terminal control areas:

   a. Traffic clearance is required prior to flight in a TCA.

   b. Student flights are prohibited.

   c. An operable two-way radio for communicating with ATC is required.

90

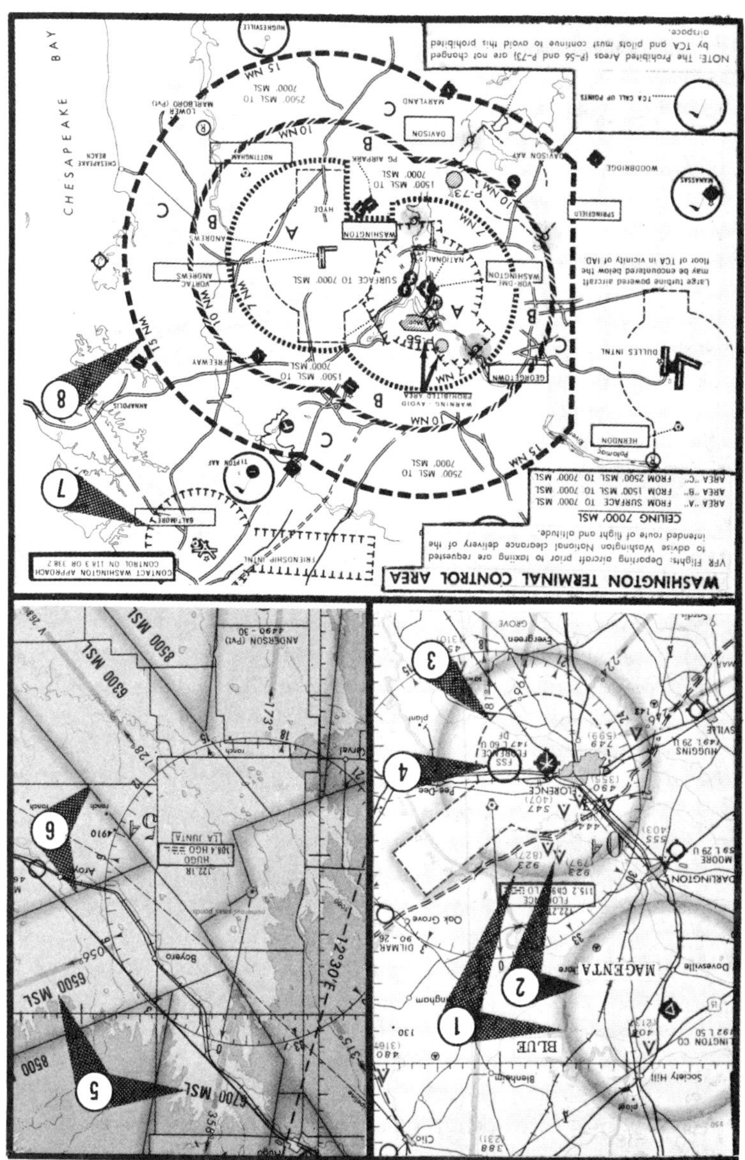

1-Control Areas (Blue Shading), 2-Transition Areas (Magenta Shading), 3-Control Zone, 4-FSS Advisory Area, 5-Nonstandard Federal Airway Floors, 6-Federal Airway (lateral limits). 7-Special VFR not permitted, 8-Terminal Control Area.

d. An operable VOR (or TACAN) receiver is required.

e. An operable radar beacon transponder having at least a mode A/3, 409B-code capability, replying to A/3 interrogations is required.

Group II terminal control areas are similar in their requirements to Group I with the exception that student flight is permitted and that radar beacon transponders are not required for VFR aircraft.

The terminal control area is basically an anti-collision flight procedure. Fundamentally this is accomplished by radar control of *all aircraft* within the boundaries of a TCA. As a VFR pilot you must obtain a clearance from ATC (approach control) before entering the TCA. Be prepared to hold outside the TCA in the event traffic conditions do not permit an immediate entry. Remember that the VFR pilot still has the obligation of remaining in VFR weather conditions. Should instructions from approach control direct a pilot too close to clouds or other non-VFR weather, advise approach control immediately and obtain an amended clearance. While so doing, remain clear of all clouds and other non-VFR weather. Radar cannot see weather as you can.

IV. Special Use Airspace.

Special use airspace consists of airspace domains where airborn activity must be confined because of the specialized nature of the activity. The following describes various classes of specialized use airspace:

1. Prohibited Area

Airspace within which the flight of aircraft is not allowed for security or other reasons associated with the national welfare unless prior permission has been granted by the cognizant government authority. An example of a prohibited area is the area that encompasses the White House and the capitol buildings in Washington, D.C. Prohibited areas are also established to safeguard the forest and wildlife in the few remaining wilderness areas of the United States. Avoid all prohibited areas!

2. Restricted Area

Airspace within which flight, while not wholly prohibited, is subject to restrictions. The function of a restricted area is to confine or segregate activities considered to be hazardous to non-participating aircraft. Restricted areas denote the existence of unusual, often invisible, hazards to aircraft such as artillery firing, aerial gun-

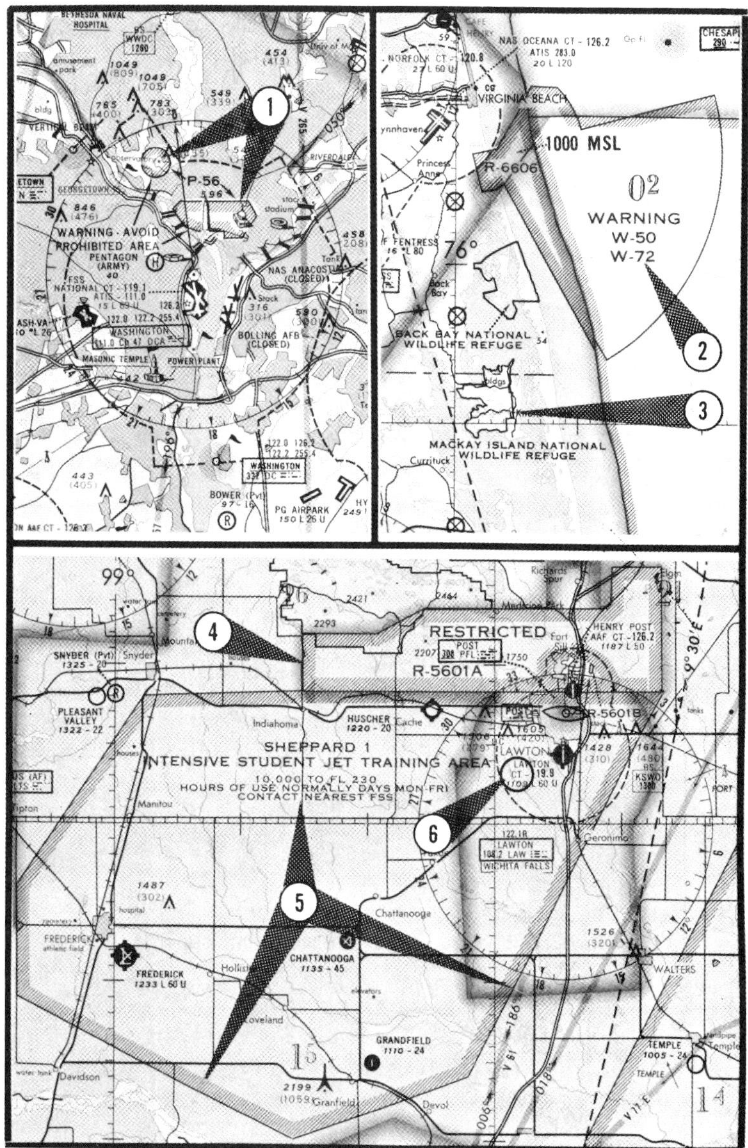

1-Prohibited Area, 2-Warning Area, 3-Wild Life Refuge, 4-Restricted Area, 5-ISTJA, 6-Control Zone and Airport Traffic Area.

nery, or guided missiles. Penetration of restricted areas without authorization from the using or controlling agency may be extremely hazardous to the aircraft and its occupants. Restricted areas vary in their hours of use. Flight information to describe a restricted area can be obtained from; (a) sectional charts, (b) by contacting Flight Service, and (c) by contacting the cognizant agency which is given authority over the restricted area in question.

3. Warning Area

A warning area is airspace, within international airspace, established to contain hazardous operations conducted by U.S. military forces. The activities conducted within warning areas may be hazardous to nonparticipating aircraft. However, no restriction to flight is imposed because flight within international airspace cannot legally be restricted. To alert nonparticipants to the existence of possible hazardous conditions, warning areas are depicted on aeronautical charts. Most warning areas lie within three statute miles of the coast line and are located over ocean areas.

4. Alert Area

Airspace which may contain a high volume of pilot training activity or an unusual type of aeronautical activity—neither of which is uncommonly hazardous to aircraft. All flight activity in an alert area shall be conducted in accordance with FAR's, without waiver, and pilots of participating aircraft as well as pilots of aircraft transiting the area shall be equally responsible for collision avoidance. The establishment of alert areas does not impose any unique flight restrictions or communications requirements. Within a control zone, the floor of an alert area is established at least 4,000 feet AGL and the ceiling no higher than the beginning of positive control airspace (18,000 feet MSL).

5. Intensive Student Jet Training Area (ISJTA)

Airspace which contains intensive flight training activities of military student jet pilots and in which restrictions are imposed on IFR flights only. All VFR flights within an ISJTA shall be conducted in accordance with FAR's without waiver, and all participating military pilots as well as pilots of aircraft transiting the area shall be equally responsible for collision avoidance. In-

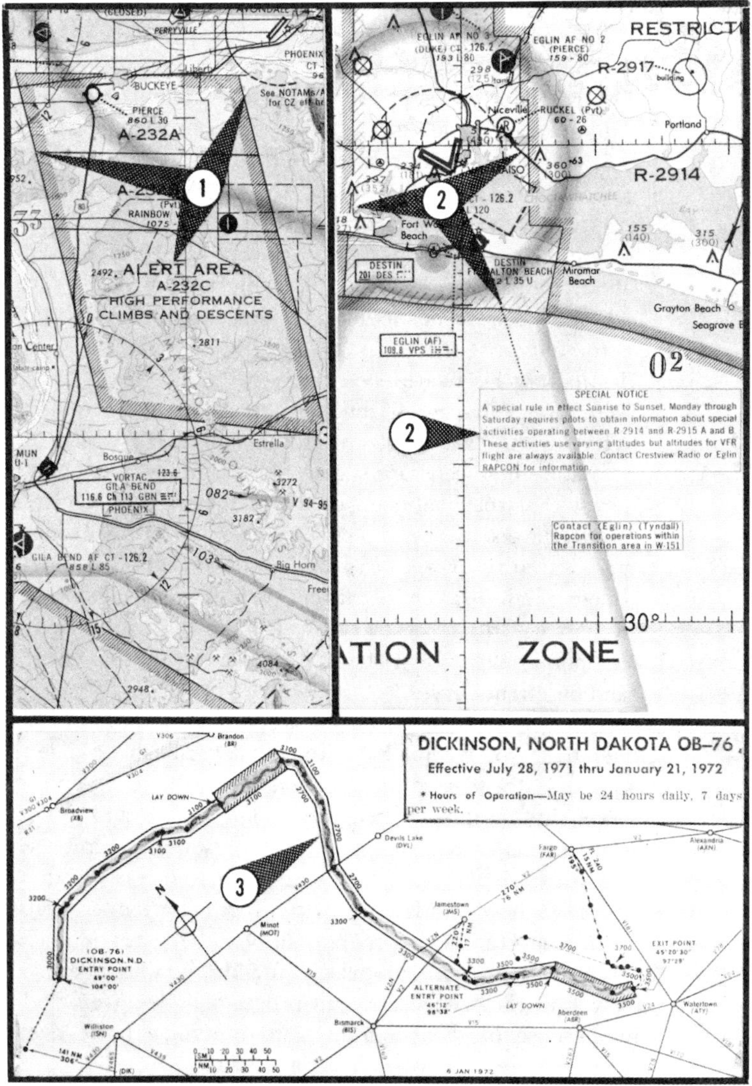

1-Alert Area, 2-Special Air Traffic Rules Area, 3-Special Operations (Olive Branch Route).

formation on training areas may be obtained from any FSS within 100 miles of the area.

6. Special Operations

Airspace which is devoted to military training routes termed Olive Branch routes. Refer to the Airmen's Information Manual Parts 3 and 4 for route descriptions. Treat these regions as alert areas.

7. Terminal Area Graphic Notice

High density terminal area suggested routes for transiting aircraft. Refer to the Airmen's Information Manual, Vol. 4, Area Notices, for route descriptions.

8. Special Air Traffic Rules and Air Traffic Patterns

Airspace in which special rules or procedures apply. For example, special rules apply to the airspace located about Valparaiso, Florida. Pilots must obtain an ATC advisory concerning operations being conducted therein before entering the area.

9. Temporary Flight Restrictions

Temporary airspace flight restrictions may be put into effect in the vicinity of any incident or event which by its nature may generate such a high degree of public interest that the likelihood of a hazardous congestion of air traffic exists. Examples are major sporting events, parades, air shows, and similar functions. Forest fires, floods, and disaster situations may likewise result in temporary flight restrictions. Information concerning temporary flight restrictions is distributed by NOTAMS and by Flight Service.

V. Voluntary Flight Procedure Airspace

Under terms of federal legislation that establishes wilderness areas, the controlling agency, be it the U.S. Forest Service, the National Park Service, or the Fish and Wildlife Service, is in a position to close or severely limit use of existing airport facilities within these areas. Rather than create new regulations to control aircraft operations in wilderness areas, a program of voluntary cooperation between the aviation community and the various agencies involved in the wilderness area program is being enacted. The purpose of the program is to minimize noise over wilderness areas; pilots are requested to "k   " while over such regions. As shown in the accompanying map of Grand Canyon National Park, areas 1 through 7

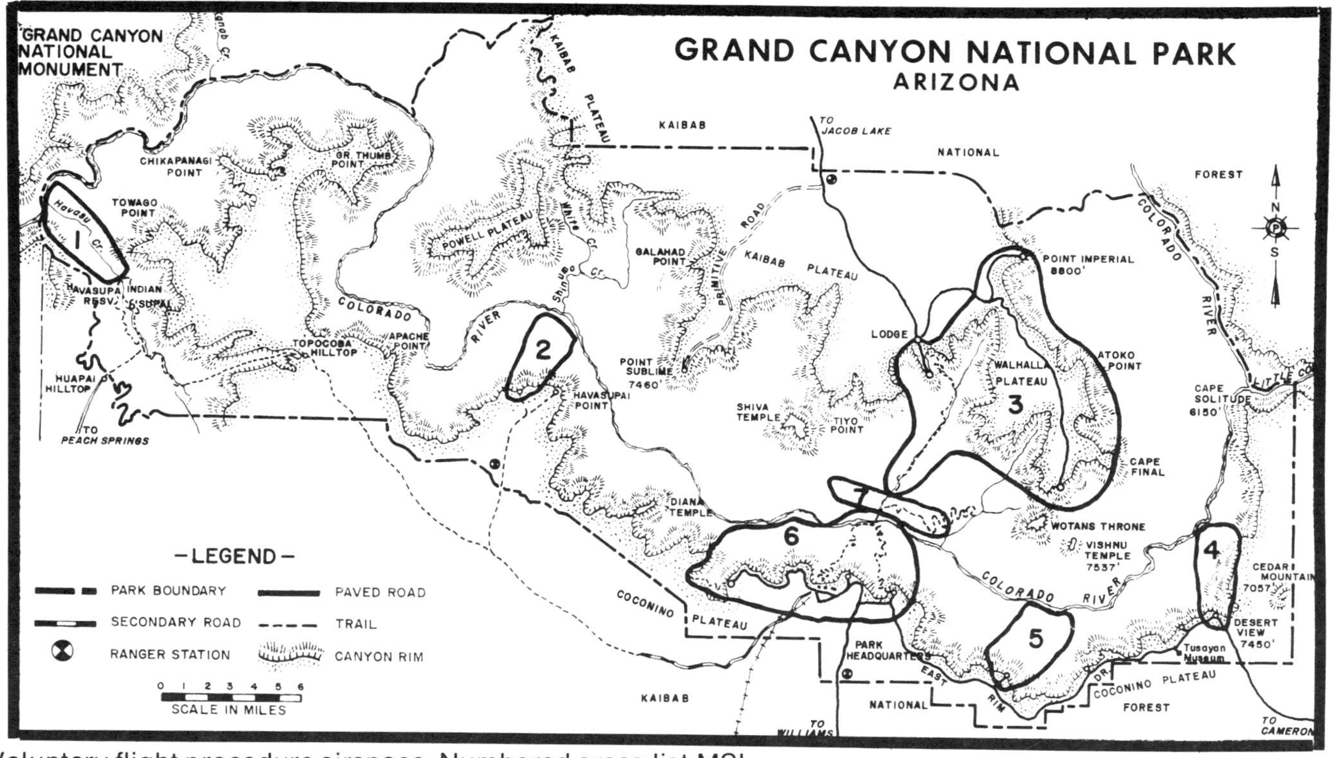

Voluntary flight procedure airspace. Numbered areas list MSL altitude minimums of: 5,000'—(1 & 5), 6,000'—(7), 6,500'—(2), 8,500'—(4, 6, and 2, 5 rim) and 10,000'—(3).

represent airspace designations where the Grand Canyon National Park Service and the FAA have instituted a program of voluntary restricted minimum altitude flight. Remember that no person is permitted to land an aircraft on land or water within an area administered by the National Park Service, except (a) at officially designated landing sites, (b) in the event of an emergency, or (c) on official business for the federal government. Should your route of flight involve a wilderness area check with your local FSS to determine voluntary procedures that may be in use. As a rule of thumb consider at least a 2,000 feet minimum AGL altitude when over-flying congested and recreational areas and national parks.

VI. Air Defense Identification Zones

Air Defense Identification Zones (ADIZ's) are areas of airspace over land or water in which the ready identification, location, and control of civil aircraft is required in the interest of national security. As shown by the accompanying map there are four such zones which surround the continental United States. These are the Pacific Coastal ADIZ, Southern Border Domestic ADIZ, Gulf of Mexico Coastal ADIZ, and Atlantic Coastal ADIZ. In addition to the ADIZ, Distant Early Warning Identification Zones (DEWIZ's) are established to provide a similar aircraft identification at long ranges. A zone of this nature is located in Alaska. If your route of flight requires the penetration of an ADIZ or DEWIZ the following regulations in general apply:

1. A flight plan is required for both VFR and IFR flight. A VFR flight plan shall be designated as DVFR.

2. Two-way radio is required for penetrating an ADIZ or DEWIZ. In the event an aircraft is not equipped with a two-way radio on a flight between Mexico and the United States, the aircraft must land at a designated airport of entry nearest the point of entry into the United States and file an arrival or a completion notice.

3. Position reports are required. DVFR flights must give their estimated time of penetration of an ADIZ at least 15 minutes before penetration takes place. DVFR aircraft entering the United States through a DEWIZ shall report before penetration takes place. Reports must contain the time, position, and altitude at which

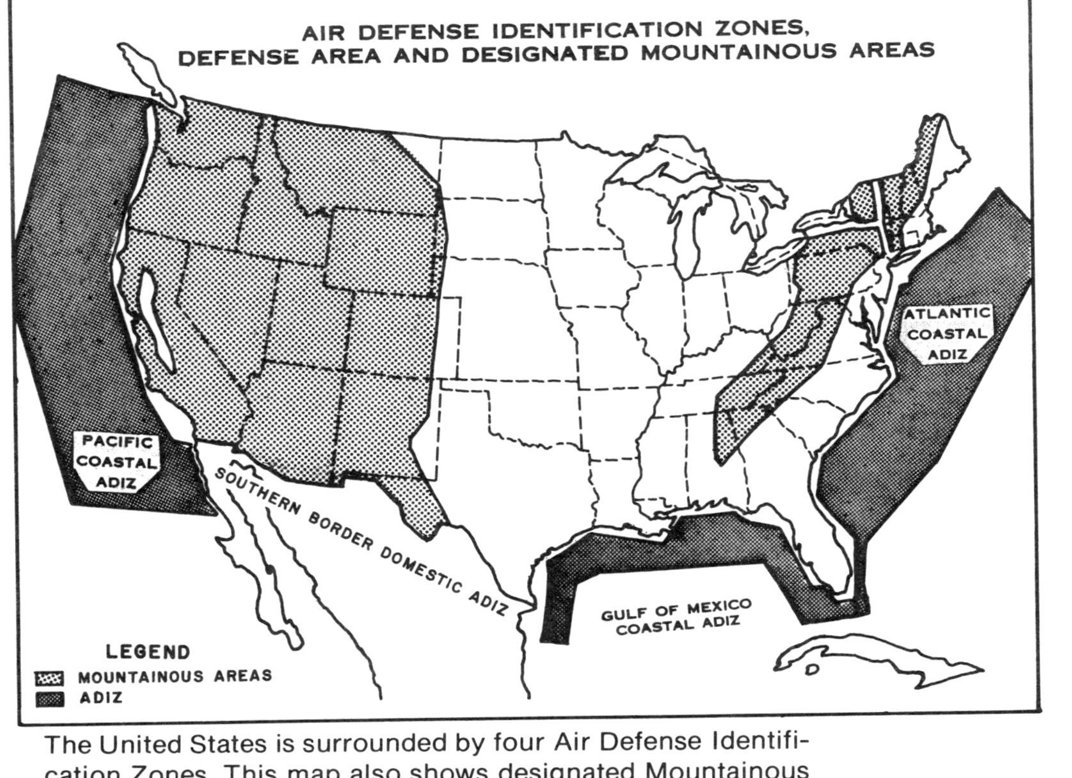

The United States is surrounded by four Air Defense Identification Zones. This map also shows designated Mountainous and Flat areas. A good altitude rule to follow is 1,000 ft. minimum over flat areas and 2,000 ft. over mountainous areas.

the aircraft passed the last reporting point before penetration and the estimated time of arrival at the next reporting point or penetration point. Time estimates should be within five minutes and course position estimates within ten miles of the center line for a domestic ADIZ and within twenty miles of course center line for a coastal ADIZ or DEWIZ.

4. With the exception of flight between Mexico and the United States, coastal or domestic ADIZ requirements do not apply if operating North of 25 degrees latitude or West of 85 degrees West longitude at a true air speed of less than 180 knots. DEWIZ procedures do not apply in Alaska when operating at a true air speed of less than 180 knots while the pilot maintains a listening watch on an appropriate frequency. ADIZ procedures do not apply within the continental United States, over or within three miles of any island in Hawaii, and for flights that remain within ten miles of a departure point.

5. In an emergency situation that requires immediate action for the safety of flight, a pilot-in-command of an aircraft may deviate from ADIZ and DEWIZ procedures to the extent required by the emergency. He must report the reasons for the deviation to the appropriate communications facility as soon as possible. In the event of radio failure an aircraft operating under a DVFR flight plan may proceed in accordance with the original flight plan or land as soon as practicable. The pilot is required to report the radio failure to the appropriate facility as soon as possible.

AIRWAY FLIGHT ROUTES

The National Airspace is divided into two major systems of airways. The airspace from surface level to 18,000 feet MSL is referred to as the low altitude structure and contains the "Victor" system of airways. The airspace from 18,000 feet MSL to flight level 600 (60,000 feet MSL on a standard day) is the high altitude structure of "Jet" airways. Fundamentally, the high altitude structure is intended to service high speed jet aircraft during the en route portions of their flight. The low altitude structure services general aviation aircraft as well as all aircraft during arrivals and descents in a terminal area. Operational differences between the Victor and Jet airways are as follows:

1. Altitudes flown on Victor airways are MSL altitudes. It is necessary for a pilot to correct his altimeter setting during the course of a flight in order to maintain a constant mean sea level altitude. Regulations require that the aircraft altimeter be set to stations along the route and within 100 nautical miles of the aircraft. If no stations are within the 100 nautical mile range an appropriate available station may be used. For aircraft not equipped with a radio, the elevation of departure airport may be employed.

2. For flights in the Jet airway system the altimeter is set to a constant *pressure altitude* of 29.92 inches of mercury. Flight in the high altitude structure is thus conducted at a constant pressure altitude instead of a constant mean sea level altitude as in the low altitude structure. Due to this fundamental difference, altitudes in the high altitude structure are referred to as flight levels. For example, flight level 190 is equivalent to 19,000 feet MSL on a standard day, flight level 200 is equivalent to 20,000 feet MSL on a standard day, etc. On non-standard days (when the altimeter is other than 29.92) flight levels will not be located at their numerically equivalent MSL altitudes. That is, flight level 190 will not be located at 19,000 feet MSL. To maintain the division between the Jet airway system and the Victor airway system at 18,000 feet MSL the lowest usable flight level is determined by the atmospheric pressure in the intended area of operation per the following table:

LOWEST USABLE FLIGHT LEVELS

Current Altimeter Setting	Lowest Usable Flight Level
29.92 (or higher)	180
29.91 thru 29.42	185
29.41 thru 28.92	190
28.91 thru 28.42	195
28.41 thru 27.92	200
27.91 thru 27.42	205
27.41 thru 26.92	210

The Jet airway system lies entirely within the region of positive control, hence all flight operations are IFR at all times.

The Hemispheric Rule

For purposes of preventing collisions between aircraft our airspace is divided into a series of layers to segregate VFR and IFR traffic as well as East bound and West bound traffic. Altitude separation between these four flight operations is in accordance with the hemispheric rule which is as follows:

VFR aircraft operating in level cruising flight at an altitude of more than 3,000 feet above the surface and less than 18,000 feet MSL shall maintain odd 1,000 foot MSL altitudes plus 500 feet when East bound (a magnetic course of zero degrees through 179 degrees) and even 1,000 foot MSL altitudes plus 500 feet when West bound (a magnetic course of 180 degrees through 359 degrees).

Who flies at the even and odd level of altitudes? That's where the IFR traffic is located in uncontrolled airspace. For East bound IFR level cruising flight below 18,000 feet typical MSL altitudes are 3,000 feet, 5,000 feet, 7,000 feet, etc. West bound IFR flights are located typically at 4,000 feet, 6,000 feet, 8,000 feet, etc. The net result is a 500 feet altitude separation between VFR and IFR traffic. Holding altitude while VFR is important!

The hemispheric rule applies at altitudes above 18,000 feet, however, since the region above 18,000 feet is positive control airspace, altitudes are assigned by ATC and flown accordingly by all pilots. In selecting your en route cruising altitude remember it's the *magnetic course* that counts (true course plus or minus magnetic variation).

Special VFR

Special VFR weather minimums allow a lower cloud clearance and visibility minimum in certain control zones if a special VFR clearance is first obtained from ATC. For fixed wing aircraft special VFR minimums are one statute mile visibility and clear of the clouds. These minimums may be determined from the cockpit except for operations to or from an airport in a control zone where ground visibility is reported. A special VFR clearance may be obtained from a control tower when such is located within a control zone. For control zones in which no control tower is located, a clearance may be obtained through the nearest tower, nearest Flight Service Station, or Air Route Traffic Control Center. It is important to remember that *special VFR is an ATC clearance.* The purpose of the clearance is to provide separation from IFR traffic or other special VFR traffic that may be in the vicinity.

Control zones that permit special VFR operations are indicated on a sectional chart by a dotted blue line. Those that do not are indicated by "T" designation. Special VFR operation is prohibited at night in all control zones unless the pilot is instrument-rated and his aircraft is IFR equipped.

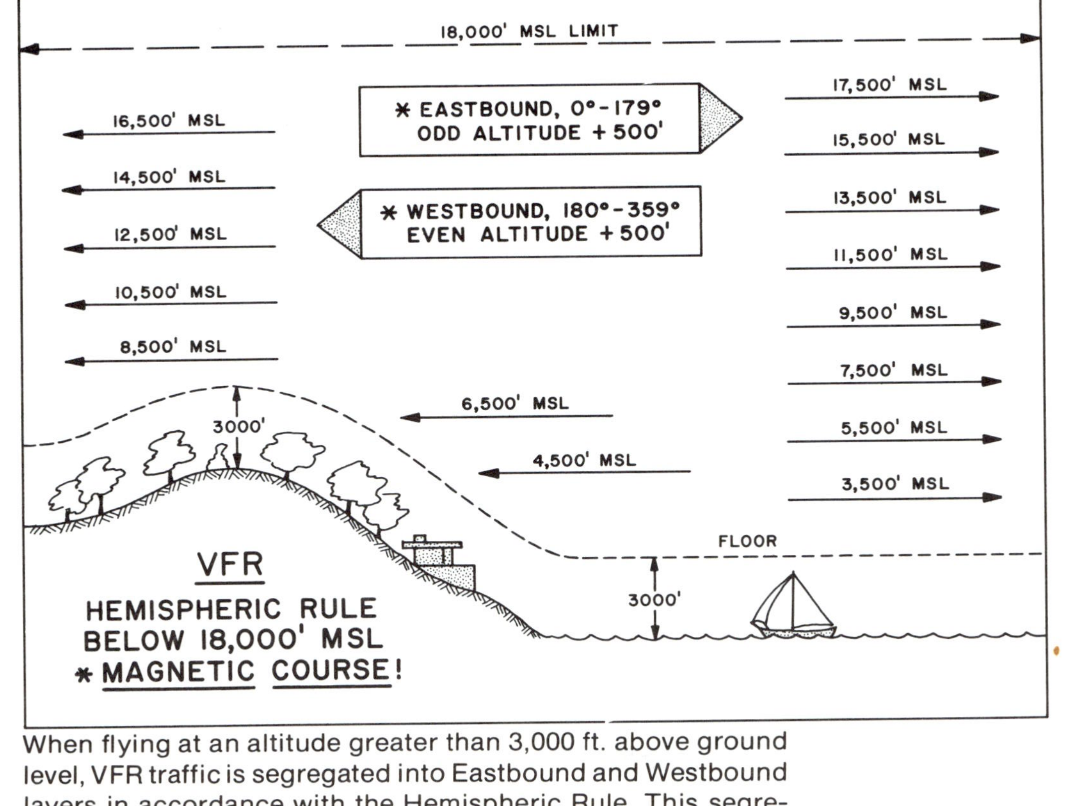

When flying at an altitude greater than 3,000 ft. above ground level, VFR traffic is segregated into Eastbound and Westbound layers in accordance with the Hemispheric Rule. This segregation is one means of collision avoidance.

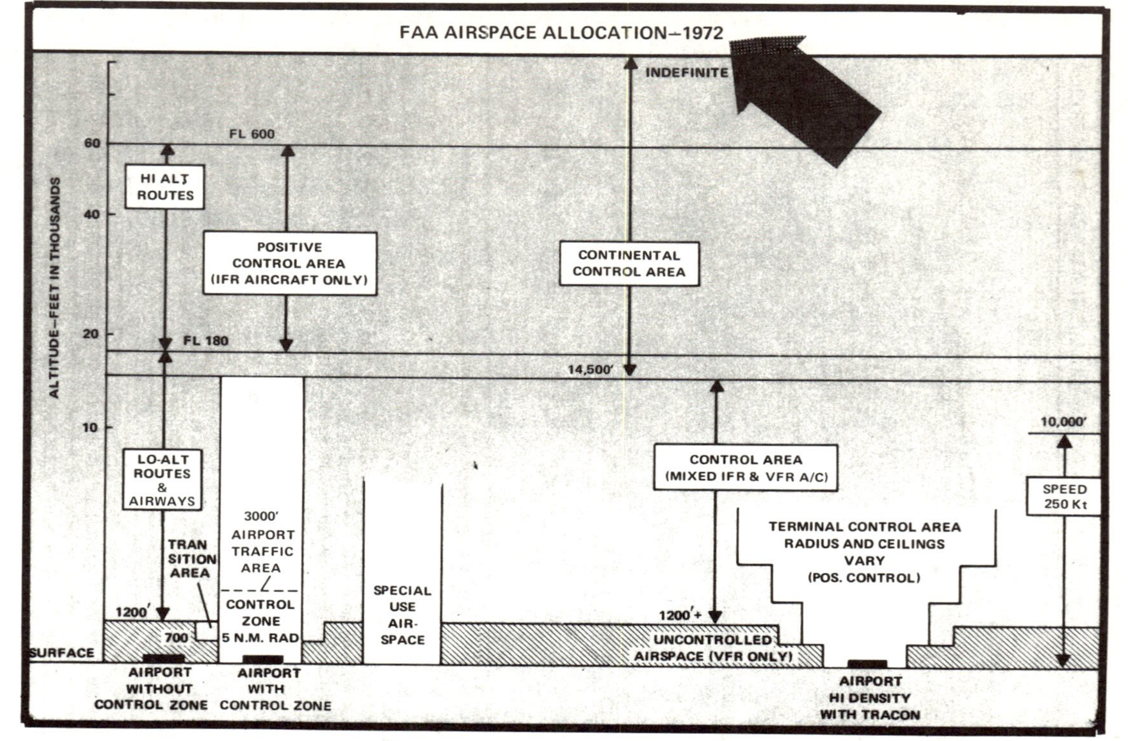

Today's airspace; positive control makes its appearance in the low altitude structure as Terminal Control Areas (TCA's).

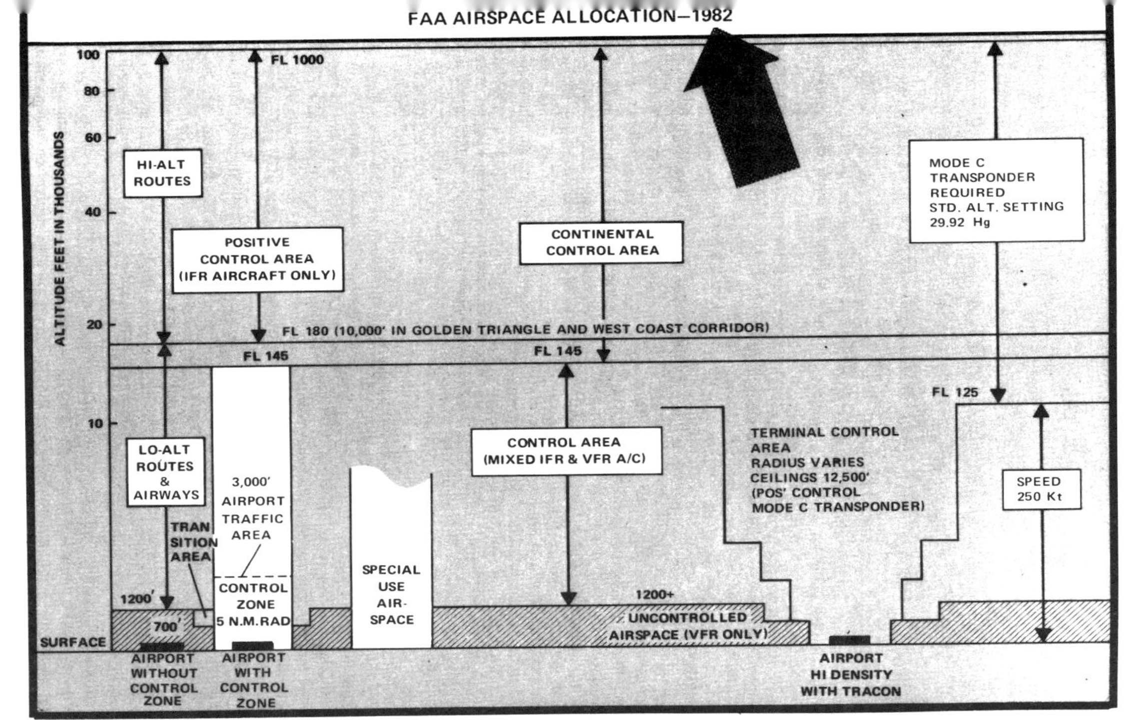

Tomorrow's airspace; increased areas of Positive control; more TCA's and a lower positive control floor in the Golden Triangle and West Coast corridor.

FUTURE AIRSPACE ALLOCATIONS AND RULES

The National Aviation System (NAS) plan for the period 1973 through 1982 notes, "In the planning period 1973-1982, the base of Area Positive Control airspace will remain at Flight Level 180 throughout most of the conterminous United States. Over some areas such as the heavily travelled routes of the Golden Triangle and on the West Coast between San Francisco and San Diego, the base will be lowered to 10,000 feet. The Golden Triangle will be redefined as that airspace within a triangle bounded by Boston, Chicago, and Atlanta. Area Positive Control will be lowered in the Golden Triangle and in the West Coast Corridor in the 1975 time frame. The use of a standard altimeter setting, 29.92" Hg. will be lowered from the present 18,000 feet to 12,500 feet MSL."

Future Terminal Control Areas will be increased in volume and in number. Current thinking is that the ceiling of the TCA airspace will be extended upward from its present limit of 7,000 feet to 12,500 feet.

CHAPTER 5—THE AIRSPACE (CONTINUED)

Part II
General Airspace Flight Rules

Federal aviation regulations provide a number of general "rules of the road" for flight within our National Airspace System. The fundamental purpose of these rules is to promote safety throughout aviation and, just as important, respect the sovereignty of the persons and property over which we fly.

MINIMUM SAFE ALTITUDES

With the exception of take-off or landing there is one overriding minimum safe altitude rule; we must fly at an altitude which will permit an emergency landing without undo hazard to persons or property on the surface if an engine(s) fails. This rule applies anywhere but is particularly important in flight over large metropolitan areas. In addition to this one basic rule, the following minimums also apply:

1. Over congested areas the minimum allowable altitude is 1,000 feet above the highest obstacle within a horizontal radius of 2,000 feet of the aircraft. The words "congested area" have not been defined in the FAR's beyond the terms city, town, settlement, or open air assembly of persons. Furthermore, enforcement cases involving charges of low-flying vary as to the definition of a congested area. As a guide, this author suggests that any group of homes greater than ten in number (or equivalent cabins, workshops, farm buildings, and the like) be considered a congested area. Remember, too, open air assemblies of persons include crowds of people lining a parade route, crowds of people in a stadium, or simply groups of people on a beach.

2. Over other than congested areas a minimum altitude of 500 feet above the surface must be maintained. As in the preceding

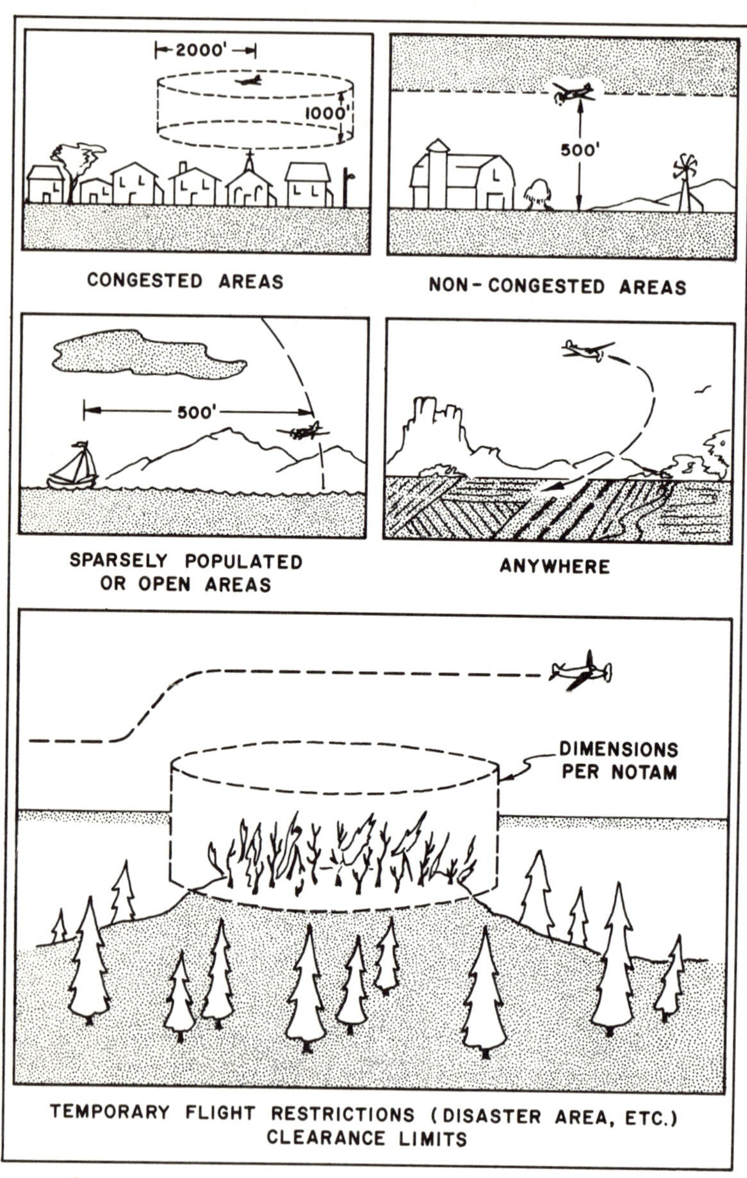

Minimum altitude clearance limits for VFR aircraft.

regulation, the phrase "other than congested areas" is not defined by FAR. The author suggests that groupings of one or two houses located a significant distance from like groupings (as in the case of open farm country) be considered "other than congested areas."

3. Over open water or sparsely populated areas aircraft may not be operated closer than 500 feet to any person, vessel, vehicle, or structure. In this instance FAR's do not imply a minimum altitude but rather a minimum distance from a structure or person. The term "sparsely populated" is interpreted herein as meaning a single isolated dwelling in the middle of a desert or a forest.

In planning a minimum altitude, an excellent guide to consider is FAR 91.119, "Minimum Altitudes for IFR operation". This regulation states in part that a minimum altitude of 2,000 feet above the highest obstacle within a horizontal distance of five statute miles from the course to be flown shall be maintained when in designated mountainous areas. In flat areas aircraft shall maintain a minimum altitude of 1,000 feet above the highest obstacle within a horizontal distance of five statute miles from the course to be flown.

RIGHT-OF-WAY RULES

The following summarizes right-of-way rules for aircraft:

1. An aircraft in distress has the right-of-way over all other air traffic.

2. When aircraft of different categories are converging the right-of-way is granted to the least maneuverable. A balloon has the right-of-way over any other category of aircraft. A glider has the right-of-way over an airship, airplane, or rotocraft. An airship has the right-of-way over an airplane or a rotocraft. An aircraft towing or refueling other aircraft has the right-of-way over all other engine driven aircraft.

3. When two aircraft are approaching each other head-on, or nearly so, each pilot of each aircraft shall alter course to the right.

4. When two aircraft are converging at approximately the same altitude at a right angle (or nearly so) the aircraft to the pilot's right has the right-of-way. This regulation is similar to the unmarked intersection in driving, that is, the auto to the right has the right-of-way. Technically speaking, a Cessna 150 would have the right-of-way over a Boeing 747 should the two be on a converging course with the 150 located to the right of the Boeing 747. While the FAR's do not differentiate in right-of-way rules applicable to light and heavy aircraft, we

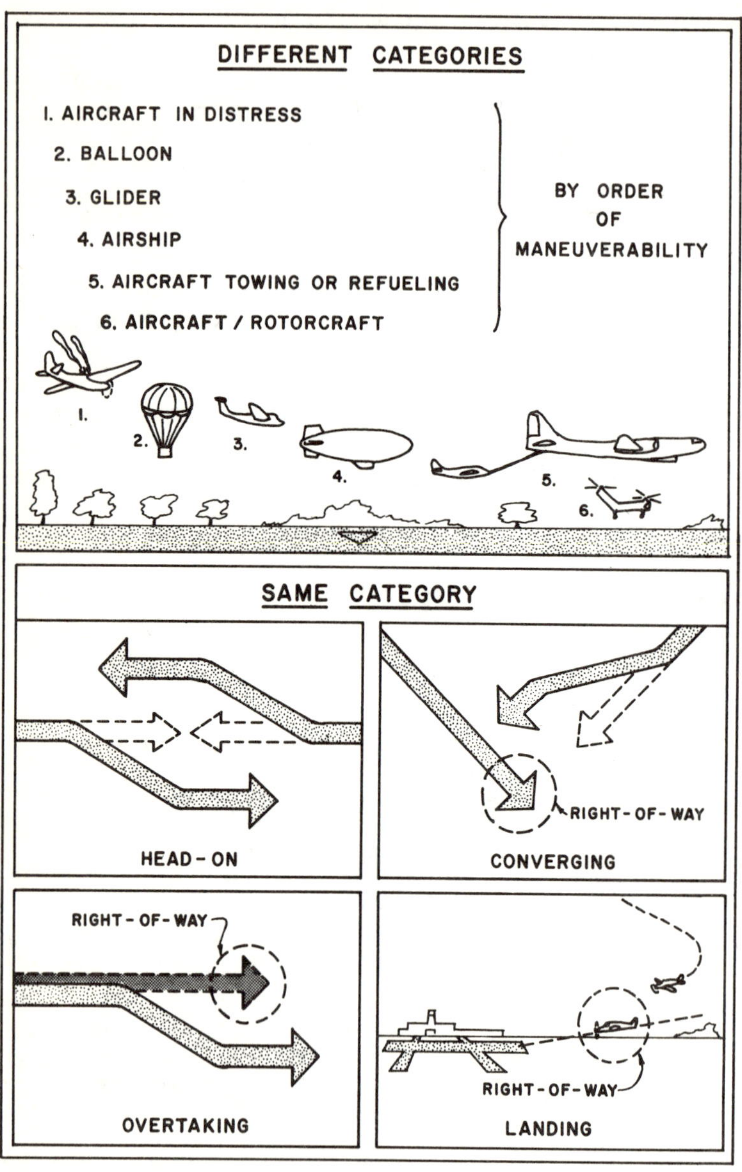

Aviation "rules of the road" for airborne vehicles of the same and different categories.

might consider the advice of Shakespeare who wrote, "The better part of valor is discretion. . . .".

5. Each aircraft that is being overtaken has the right-of-way and each pilot of an overtaking aircraft shall alter course to the right and pass well clear.

6. Aircraft, while on final approach to land, or while landing, have the right-of-way over other aircraft in flight or operating on the surface. When two or more aircraft are approaching an airport for the purpose of landing, the aircraft at the lower altitude has the right-of-way, but it shall not take advantage of this rule to cut in front of another which is on final approach to land, or to overtake that aircraft.

7. Aircraft operating over water shall, insofar as possible, keep clear of all vessels and avoid impeding their navigation.

8. When an aircraft and a vessel are approaching head-on or nearly so, each shall alter its course to the right and keep well clear.

9. When an aircraft and a vessel are on crossing courses, the aircraft or vessel to the other's right has the right-of-way.

10. An aircraft or vessel that is being overtaken has the right-of-way, and the one overtaking shall alter course to keep well clear.

ACROBATIC FLIGHT

Acrobatic flight is not permitted over any congested area of a city, town, or settlement or over an open air assembly of persons. In addition, such is not permitted within a control zone or federal airway. The minimum altitude for acrobatic flight is 1,500 feet above the surface and the minimum flight visibility is three statute miles.

FORMATION FLIGHT

Formation flight is not permitted except by previous arrangement with the pilot-in-command of each aircraft in the formation. Carrying passengers for hire in formation flight is not permitted. A pilot flying in formation must not operate his aircraft so close to another as to create a collision hazard.

CARELESS OR RECKLESS OPERATIONS

A person may not operate an aircraft in the air or on the ground in a careless or reckless manner so as to endanger the life or property of another. No pilot-in-command may allow any object to be dropped from that aircraft in flight that creates a hazard to persons or property. (Objects may be dropped if reasonable precautions are taken to avoid injury or damage to persons or property).

LIQUOR AND DRUGS

No person may act as a crew member of a civil aircraft within eight hours after the consumption of any alcoholic beverage, while under the influence of alcohol, or while using any drugs that affect his faculties in any way contrary to safety. Furthermore, except in an emergency, no pilot may allow a person who is obviously under the influence of intoxicating liquors or drugs (except a medical patient under proper care) to be carried in that aircraft.

FLIGHTS BETWEEN MEXICO AND THE UNITED STATES

No person may operate a civil aircraft between Mexico and the United States, with knowledge that narcotic drugs, marijuana, or depressant or stimulant drugs or substances as defined in federal statutes are carried in the aircraft. Furthermore, persons operating a civil aircraft between Mexico and the United States must comply with requirements for penetrating the ADIZ as noted in Part I of this chapter. If the aircraft does not have a two-way radio, that person shall, in addition to complying to ADIZ requirements, land at the designated airport of entry nearest the point of entry into the United States, and file an arrival or completion notice.

Looking toward the future, stiffer anti-drug regulations are predicted. It is currently proposed that FAA be granted the authority to suspend or revoke, as well as deny application for, pilot certificates and/or operating certificates of all persons convicted of violating any federal or state statute, "relating to the growing, processing, manufacturing, sale, disposition, possession, transportation or importation of narcotic drugs, marijuana, and depressant or stimulant drugs or substances." In addition, it is proposed that mandatory flight plans be required for persons operating a civil aircraft on a flight between Mexico or Canada and the United States.

Many countries, including Canada and Mexico, require advance notice of the intent of pilots to arrive in those countries. Under agreements between the United States, Canada, and Mexico, operators of private planes may, in most cases, include this advance notice in a flight plan to be filed prior to departure from the United States with the nearest FAA communications station. The station will then relay the message to the proper authorities in the country of destination without further action on the part of the pilot. In a similar manner operators of private planes upon reentering the United States from a foreign country must provide an advance notice of the estimated time of arrival *to U.S. Customs for each flight.* In general, one hour advance notice is sufficient. Advance notice may be provided by a direct phone call to Customs, by filing a flight plan with a request to "advise customs," or by radio contact with the nearest Flight Service Station after take-off. For Customs services Sundays, holidays, or outside regular duty hours expect to be charged an overtime fee, payable in cash. For detailed information on customs regulations contact your local FSS or write for the following booklet:

> Customs Guide for Private Flyers
> Stock No. 4802-0029, Price $.25
> Superintendent of Documents
> U.S. Government Printing Office
> Washington, D.C. 20402

AIRCRAFT LIGHTING

Regulations require that aircraft position lights be turned on from official sunset to official sunrise. This applies regardless of whether the aircraft is in flight or taxiing on the ground. The aircraft anti-collision rotating beacon or strobe light is likewise required to be turned on. Hours for sunset and sunrise can be determined by calling FSS, tower, or other such ATC facility. Tables of sunrise and sunset are available for almost all cities of over 50,000 population. To obtain information on your particular city request a table of sunrise and sunset times from the following agency:

> Nautical Almanac Office
> United States Naval Observatory
> Washington, D.C. 20390

For those in Alaska, aircraft position lights must additionally be turned on during periods when a prominent unlighted object cannot be seen from a distance of three statute miles or when the sun is more than six degrees below the horizon.

COMPLIANCE WITH
ATC CLEARANCES

When a pilot requests and is granted an air traffic control clearance there exists, in effect, a verbal contract between the pilot and the air traffic controller. The contract is "signed" when the pilot acknowledges and accepts the ATC clearance. Each contract (clearance and acknowledgment) so formed is unique; it exists be-

As aviation grows additional dependence will be placed on ARTS II and III facilities (Automated Terminal Radar Service) for both IFR *and* VFR flight. Radar traffic advisory, vectoring, and sequencing service in the vicinity of sizeable airports is a highly desirable VFR procedure. A call to radar 15-25 miles out is all that is required to obtain service.

(Photo courtesy of FAA)

tween the *individual* pilot and his air traffic controller. A clearance given to one pilot does not apply to another even though their situations may be similar. Furthermore, when an ATC clearance has been obtained, no pilot-in-command may deviate from that clearance, except in an emergency, unless he obtains an amended clearance.

Emergency Authority of the Pilot-in-Command

FAR 91.3 grants a pilot-in-command emergency authority; that is, authority to deviate from flight rules in an emergency to the extent required to meet that emergency. What constitutes an emergency? The situations are many and varied. A few examples follow:

1. Getting caught in a weather situation that puts a VFR pilot in an IFR situation.

2. Night flight can provide unexpected experiences for the low-time VFR pilot. On a dark night clouds are not visible, distant auto headlights and stars appear similar, and the horizon is often indistinct if visible at all. IFR situations may exist even though VFR conditions prevail.

3. Unexpected illness on the part of the pilot or a passenger.

4. A failure of the aircraft power plant or instruments that would affect the safety of the flight.

114

5. Becoming lost or disoriented.

6. Low on fuel.

Whatever the situation, uncertainty, alert, or distress, three basic actions by the pilot-in-command will bring the ATC network to his assistance. First, if transponder equipped, squawk Code 7700. This rings bells and lights at all ATC radar facilities within range. In addition, your radar return signal is automatically identified thus giving the radar controller your location. Second, contact the air traffic control agency nearest you (FSS, tower, center, etc.). If unable to determine the appropriate frequency, use the emergency frequency 121.5 MHz. Identify who you are, where you are, the nature of the distress, and the type of assistance desired. Advise ATC that you are "declaring an emergency." This will grant you priority over other aircraft under ATC control in your local area. Third, comply with advice and instructions received.

When a pilot is in doubt of his position, or feels apprehensive for his safety, he should not hesitate to request assistance. Search and rescue facilities, including radar, radio, and Direction Finding stations are ready and willing to help. There is no penalty for using this service. Delay in so doing has caused accidents and cost lives. A pilot-in-command who is given priority by ATC in an emergency, *if requested,* shall submit a detailed report of that emergency within 48 hours to the chief of the particular ATC facility involved.

SPEED LIMITS

The following aircraft speed limits apply:

1. Surface to 10,000 feet MSL: 250 knots maximum.

2. Below layers of a Terminal Control Area: 200 knots maximum.

3. Within an airport traffic area: 156 knots—reciprocating engine aircraft, 200 knots—jet aircraft. If located within a TCA, 250 knots—all aircraft.

Military aircraft which cannot slow to the specified speeds are permitted to operate at safe minimum speeds for the type of aircraft involved.

LANDING AREAS

With over 12,000 public airports there is little doubt that such is the intended terminal area for aircraft. Landing at private or restricted airports is subject to conditions that may be imposed by the owner. Furthermore, airports of this nature often do not meet national standards for over-runs, obstacles, and other conditions which may make landings and take-offs hazardous. The FAA does not have jurisdiction over such airports.

Except in an emergency, a landing in open country is open to question. In a national park or wildlife preserve the regulations previously noted apply. On municipal or state-owned property conditions imposed by the cognizant government body apply. Some states prohibit landing in open country except in the case of an emergency. Consult your local FAA GADO *and state aviation authority* regarding landing in areas other than at public airports.

CHAPTER 6
ACCIDENT REPORTS
AND INVESTIGATIONS

The National Transportation and Safety Board was established as a part of the FAA Act of 1958 to make rules and regulations governing the notification and reporting of accidents involving civil aircraft and to investigate such accidents and report the facts and probable cause. The Board is responsible to recommend to the FAA actions designed to prevent similar accidents in the future, issue reports to the public where such will enhance safety, and determine techniques or procedures that will eliminate or reduce the possibility of accidents. The primary function of the NTSB is to promote safety in transportation. A second function of the NTSB is to review airmen appeals relating to suspension, amendment, revocation, or denial of certificates (such as pilot's certificate).

The NTSB delegates authority to the FAA to investigate certain aircraft accidents and to submit reports to the Board from which the NTSB may determine the probable cause of the accident. Authority is granted the FAA to investigate and furnish reports to the NTSB on (1) all non-fatal general aviation aircraft accidents; (2) all aerial application accidents; (3) all amateur-built aircraft accidents; and (4) all restricted category aircraft accidents. In addition, the FAA is granted authority to investigate and report on fixed-wing aircraft accidents for vehicles which are not engaged in air carrier or air taxi operations and weigh less than 12,500 pounds.

The NTSB establishes rules pertaining to aircraft accidents, incidents, over-due aircraft, and safety investigations. The operator of an aircraft is required to immediately notify the National Transportation Safety Board, Bureau of Aviation Safety Field Office in case of any of the following aircraft accidents or incidents:

1. Aircraft accidents;

2. Flight control system malfunction or failure;

3. Inability of any required flight crew member to perform his normal flight duties as a result of injury or illness;

As the Number I selling retractable, the Piper Cherokee Arrow II carries a 200 hp Lycoming and cruises at 165 mph with four persons aboard. Useful load is 1,151 lbs.
(Photo courtesy of Piper Aircraft Corp.)

The Piper Aztec E, a stretched version, cruises at 210 mph with normally aspirated 250 hp engines and 245 mph with turbocharged power plants. Since its introduction, this aircraft has consistently been among top-selling twin-engine airplanes.
(Photo courtesy of Piper Aircraft Corp.)

4. Turbine engine rotor failures excluding compresser blades and turbine buckets;

5. In-flight fire;

6. Aircraft collide in flight;

7. An aircraft is overdue and is believed to have been involved in an accident.

The notification shall include the following information if available:

a. Type, nationality, and registration marks of the aircraft;

b. Name of owner, and operator of aircraft;

c. Name of the Pilot-in-command;

d. Date and time of accident;

e. Last point of departure and point of intended landing of the aircraft;

f. Postion of the aircraft with reference to some easily defined geographical point;

g. Number of persons aboard, number killed and number seriously injured;

h. Nature of the accident including weather and the extent of damage to the aircraft so far as it is known;

i. A description of any explosives, radioactive materials, or other dangerous articles carried.

The NTSB may be notified through the local FAA office or, in major cities, by direct telephone contact with the NTSB field office.

A formal report is required within ten days after an accident or reportable incident has occurred; or when after seven days an overdue aircraft is still missing. An "aircraft accident" means an occurrence associated with the operation of an aircraft which takes place between the time any person boards the aircraft with the intention of flight until such time as all such persons have disembarked. An accident is defined as a situation in which any persons suffered death or serious injury as a result of being in an aircraft or by direct contact with the aircraft or anything attached thereto, or the aircraft received substantial damage. "Fatal injuries" imply any injury which results in death within seven days. A "serious injury" means any injury which (1) requires hospitalization for more than 48 hours, commencing within seven days from the date the injury was received; (2) results in a fracture of any bone (except simple fractures of fingers, toes, or nose); (3) involves lacerations which cause severe hemorrhages, nerve, muscle, or tendon damage; (4) involves injury to any internal organ; or (5) involves second-or third-degree burns, or any burns affecting more than 5% of the body surface. The term "substantial damage" implies aircraft damage which adversely affects structural strength, performance, or flight characteristics of the aircraft resulting in a major repair.

The preceding paragraph, although long and involved to read, has been included to reinforce the responsibility associated with being a pilot-in-command.

A report on an incident for which notification is required shall be filed *only if requested* by a representative of the NTSB. "Incidents" are many and varied. Typically incidents relate to simple engine failure, bent fairings or cowlings, dented skin, ground damage to propeller blades, damage to landing gear, wheels, tires, flaps, engine accessories, brakes, wing tips, etc.

In summary, NTSB regulations require immediate notification in cases of major accidents or overdue aircraft with formal reports following ten days after an accident and seven days after an overdue aircraft is still missing. Reports on incidents are only filed if requested. NTSB Form 6120.1, is the proper document for filing an aircraft accident report for small aircraft (under 12,500 pounds).

CHAPTER 7
ENFORCEMENT PROCEDURES

Under Title IX of the Federal Aviation Act of 1958, FAA is granted authority to enforce regulations and levy penalties for both civil and criminal actions. Safety, economic, and postal offenses are subject to civil penalties; perjury of certificates, false marking of aircraft, interference with air navigation, falsification of records, transportation of dangerous articles, aircraft piracy, carrying weapons aboard an aircraft, and the like are subject to criminal penalties. In enacting the Federal Aviation Act of 1958, Congress granted the FAA and the NTSB authority to investigate violations, hold hearings, subpoena witnesses, collect evidence, and levy penalties commensurate with the violation. Thus the FAA and NTSB become successively the first two levels in a system of "courts" applicable to aviation. Cases that are appealed beyond the NTSB level enter the federal district court as the third level in the hierarchy of justice. At this point and beyond legal proceedings are conducted in a traditional fashion.

Any person who knows of a violation of the Federal Aviation Act of 1958, or of any regulation or order issued under it may report it to an FAA regional or district office. Each report is investigated by FAA personnel. The results of that investigation are the basis for determining enforcement actions that the FAA will take.

MINOR VIOLATIONS

If it is found that a violation does not require legal enforcement action, a flight standards inspector or other appropriate FAA official may issue a safety compliance notice including a letter of reprimand to the violator, or a letter of correction that confirms decisions and states the corrective action agreed to as acceptable to the FAA. If the agreed upon corrective action is successfully completed, the case is terminated. If, however, the agreed upon corrective action is not successfully completed, legal enforcement action may be initiated.

Let us take an example to examine the process involved. Assume that a non-instrument rated private pilot carrying passen-

A plane that rivals the Skyhawk in popularity, the Cessna Skylane/182 is built to carry four persons and baggage in comfort. With a cruise speed of 160 mph, a useful load of 1,305 lbs., and a range of 910 miles, the Skylane is a fine cross-country machine.

(Photo courtesy of Cessna Aircraft Co.)

The Piper Cherokee Six is available with either 260 or 300 hp Lycoming power plants. Optimum cruise is 158 mph with 260 hp and 168 mph with 300 hp. The useful load ranges from 1,601 to 1,694 lbs. depending upon power plant option.

(Photo courtesy of Piper Aircraft Corp.)

gers gets "caught" in IFR conditions and requests help by declaring an emergency. Further assume that the pilot is current in the aircraft, possesses a valid medical, and has done an average job of checking weather prior to flight. Although he was either unfortunate or possibly wrong in proceeding into IFR conditions he was absolutely right in declaring an emergency. By so doing he correctly considered the welfare of his passengers and also other aircraft that might legally be IFR in the local vicinity. After landing, most likely the following procedural actions would occur.

First the FAA gathers the relevant facts of the matter. Who is the pilot-in-command? What is the status of his medical? Who owns the aircraft? What was the history of the flight (and flight planning)? What weather briefing information was available en route? Were all charts current? The facts are assembled to answer the basic question, "was the emergency of the pilot's own making or did it occur as a result of an unforecast weather situation?"

At this point, the FAA has discretionary authority. Assuming that the emergency was not of the pilot's own making, an informal discussion of the matter with an FAA accident prevention specialist may terminate the issue. Let us assume that the pilot was found to be a trifle careless. He may then be requested to brush up by taking some ground school work or he may be required to take a written and/or flight test reexamination if there is evidence of incompetence.

Should it be determined that the pilot was truly negligent— the emergency was of his own making—he may be subject to suspension of his flying privileges for a period of time or a fine (but not both).

In general it may be stated that the investigative-enforcement action resulting from a violation of regulations is conducted from the standpoint of positive motivation. A serious and detailed effort is made to determine the underlying cause of a regulatory violation. Counseling and/or a review of aeronautical requirements and practices is first accomplished. Should reprimand be required, as in the case of repeated FAR violations by a pilot, the fine or certificate suspension is tailored to the individual, and the violation involved. For persons who make their living by flying, a fine may be levied so as not to jeopardize their occupation through suspension of their certificate. Conversely, for persons who are of financial means or fly for sport, the removal of their pilot privileges for a period of time is often the more meaningful reprimand.

SERIOUS VIOLATIONS

Serious violations of Federal Aviation Regulations are subject to legal enforcement actions and penalties. Violations of civil matters such as the nationality and ownership of aircraft, safety regulations, or aircraft access investigations are subject to penalties of $1,000 for each violation. If such violation is a continuing one, each day of the violation may constitute a separate offense. If a civil penalty is considered advisable by the FAA, a formal letter is sent to the person charged with the violation, advising him of the charges against him and the law, regulation, or order that he is charged with violating and, if appropriate, an offer to compromise the penalty. The person charged with the violation may present, to the official who signed the letter any oral or written material or information in answer to the charges, explaining, mitigating, or denying the violation or showing extenuating circumstances. Material or information so presented is considered in making final determination as to probable liability for a civil penalty, or the amount for which it will be compromised. If the person charged with the violation offers to compromise for a specific amount, he may send a certified check or money order for that amount payable to the Federal Aviation Administration. Assuming the compromise amount is acceptable the person charged with the violation is notified, by letter, that the acceptance is full settlement of the civil penalty for the violation. If the compromise settlement is not acceptable the FAA may instigate proceedings to collect the penalty.

As another form of enforcement procedure the FAA may reinspect any civil aircraft or reexamine any civil airman at any time. In cases where the FAA is considering the suspension or removal of a pilot's certificate, the pilot will be advised of the charges and the proposed action by letter. The letter, a notice of proposed certificate action, allows the holder to answer the charges by checking the appropriate box on the form. The holder may thus:

1. Admit the charges and surrender his certificate;

2. Answer the charges in writing;

3. Request an order be issued in accordance with the notice of proposed certificate action so that he may appeal to the National Transportation Safety Board;

4. Request an opportunity to be heard in an informal conference with the FAA council; or

5. Request a formal hearing if the charges concern a matter under Title V of the Act (Nationality and Ownership of aircraft).

A four to six place, twin-engine, high performance, turbo-charged, pressurized monoplane, the Beech Duke A60 is an aircraft built for operation in positive control airspace. With a service ceiling over 30,000 ft. and a cruise speed of 271 mph at 25,000 ft., this aircraft spells fast transport.

(Photo courtesy of Beech Aircraft Corp.)

The holder must return the form with his answer not later than 15 days after the date it is received, otherwise the FAA will issue the certificate action as proposed. If the holder has requested an informal conference with the FAA council and the charges concern nationality and ownership of aircraft, he may after that conference also request a formal hearing in writing by letter with postmark not later than ten days after the close of the conference. A formal hearing is conducted in the manner of a trial court with the hearing officer acting as the judge. Witnesses are called and testify under oath, motions are allowed, and parties are given an opportunity to present arguments usually through an attorney. The hearing officer listens to the evidence and makes the final judgment as to whether the airman's certificate should be amended, suspended, or revoked.

In the event a person is not satisfied with the results of a hearing, he may file an appeal with the National Transportation and Safety Board for a retrial. Where possible, hearings with the FAA or NTSB will be held at a federal facility near the home location of the accused so as to minimize travel on the part of persons involved. Should a ceetificate holder believe the action of the FAA to be unreasonable, arbitrary, or contrary to law *after* he has exhausted his right of appeal to the NTSB, he may then appeal to a federal district court for further retrial.

Penalties for serious crimes range from seizure of the aircraft to a fine of $1,000 and/or three years imprisonment for forgery of certificates and false marking of aircraft; a $5,000 fine and/or five years imprisonment for interference with air navigation; $10,000 fine and/or ten years imprisonment for illegal transportation of explosives and other dangerous articles, and twenty years imprisonment or death* for aircraft piracy.

Serious violations require the FAA initiate a thorough investigation of *all* facts involved. Not only are the aeronautical data of the accident investigated but related civil facts are assembled. Has the airman ever been cited for a criminal violation? Does he have any record of misdemeanors? What is his driving record? What is his exact medical history? Is a possible psychological problem involved? The set of data so assembled is accomplished with exceeding thoroughness to provide a case that will withstand a test of the courts. Facts relating to both the guilt *and the innocence* of the accused are assembled. A report is filed with the FAA regional office and the legal procedural machinery is put into action.

Of course, results depend upon the details of a situation. To illustrate, let us assume a pilot-in-command is involved in an aircraft accident for which alcoholic impairment of efficiency and judgement was the cause.** The nature of the reprimand? Probable revocation of the pilot's certificate for at least a year. At the end of the revocation period the pilot may apply to have his certificate reinstated. However, he may be required to *retake all of the medical, written, and flight test examinations applicable to his certificate* in order to gain reinstatement! Should there be indications that problems leading to the accident continue to persist, it is most likely that the FAA will not grant a reinstatement; the pilot may be denied his certificate for an additional period of time.

Fundamentally, it is not the policy of the FAA to discipline through revocation of a pilot's certificate. Rather, the matter is to ground the violator until the fundamental cause factor can be overcome; perhaps by additional training; perhaps by medical aid; or by requiring a "breather" to reevaluate one's outlook on flight safety. With the problem area overcome, reinstatement of a pilot's

---

*Per the FAA Act of 1958; subject to current court decisions relating to capital punishment.

**Typically 44 fatal accidents per year.

126

certificate is likely provided the airman can demonstrate that he meets the aeronautical standards required. Is the procedure effective? It must be for the FAA has a record of fewer repeat violators than any other comparable regulatory agency.

CONCLUSION

We have dealt in this chapter with enforcement procedures from the standpoint of the federal government. However, this is but a part of the story. Violations which result in property damage or bodily injury may be compounded by additional legal action. Personal liability law suits may well extract an enforcement penalty far greater than that levied by the federal government.

In conclusion, let us remember *the law represents the minimum limit of acceptability that society will condone.* Enforcement results when that limit is exceeded.

Good luck and good flying.

The End